THE LITTLE BOOK OF

ADVENT

DAILY WISDOM FROM THE WORLD'S GREATEST SPIRITUAL TEACHERS

COMPILED BY

✤

ARTHUR HOWELLS

D1016120

To Margaret with love and gratitude

First published in 2015 by William Collins
An imprint of HarperCollins*Publishers*
1 London Bridge Street,
London, SE1 9GF

WilliamCollinsBooks.com

Scripture quotations in each day's 'Scripture Reading' section
are taken from the New Revised Standard Version Bible,
copyright © 1989 by the Division of Christian Education of the
National Council of the Churches of Christ in the USA,
and are used by permission. All rights reserved.

Arthur Howells asserts the moral right to be
identified as the compiler of this work.

A catalogue record for this book is available
from the British Library.

ISBN 978-0-00-814079-3

Printed and bound in Great Britain by
Clays Ltd, St Ives plc.

MIX
Paper from
responsible sources
FSC C007454

CONTENTS

The Third Week of Advent

The Fourth Week of Advent

FOREWORD

In every Christian life there are people who have been signposts for us on the journey; when I was young in ministry, Arthur Howells was one such signpost. Just as I valued his counsel then, so I value this wonderfully 'catholic' collection of readings, reflections and prayers today.

The Church-English Dictionary[1] defined Advent as 'From the Latin *Ad Verso*, which means "To crowd out God before Christmas with activities of dubious worth".' There's some truth in that.

'Advent' is one of those words that is slipping out of common use, but it is pregnant with meaning. These four weeks are not simply a run-up to 25 December, a hectic dash between carol services and office parties up to a particular deadline, but a season in which to be taken by surprise. Advent evokes those uncertain, frustrating, exciting weeks of final expectation before a birth, days to stay close to the 'phone, to make sure there's fuel in the car and to act on the call when it comes.

The journey through Advent, short as it is, can seem like a race, but if we slow down for long enough every day this little book will provide signposts from the Scriptures, from the wisdom of the sages and with prayer to

---

[1] Martin Wroe, Adrian Reith and Simon Parkes (Kingsway, 1991).

point us towards the Babe of Bethlehem who is the eternal Word of God.

Having used *The Little Book of Lent* in prayer with my colleagues, it is a great privilege to be invited to commend this book, which I do most warmly. It is my hope and prayer that the coming Saviour will surprise us all in our Advent journey to him.

+Robert Sodor as Mannin.

+ROBERT SODOR AS MANNIN
THIE YN ASPICK
ISLE OF MAN

INTRODUCTION

The four weeks before Christmas, the season of Advent, are full of joy and anticipation as we await the coming of Jesus. Just as Lent prepares us for Easter, so Advent is a time for getting ready for Christmas. The purpose of this little book is to help us to reflect on the Advent theme. It is hoped that these reflections will encourage us to ponder the meaning of Christ's coming, living as we do in the busy, puzzled world of today. We are about to celebrate the birthday of Christ. Every birthday symbolises a new beginning, so let's prepare for the celebration of this special birthday of God's Son with expectancy and hope.

How are we going to use this book? At this time of year we tend to be caught up in a frenetic busyness! There seems little time to do anything apart from buying presents, sending cards, decorating the tree and planning the Christmas dinner. Here is a well-tried and effective way that may help you as you make your Advent journey. Try setting aside some time each day to look at the Bible passage and the reflection and to enter into a dialogue with God. After settling down in stillness and silence you may like to read the Bible passage first. You may find that you need to read the verses through slowly and repeatedly. Now turn to the extract which provides a commentary or angle on the Scripture reading. Again read this slowly and carefully a few times and see how you react to what is written. Finally turn all this into prayer using the prayer printed at the end of the passage or your own words to express what you want to say to God.

I am most grateful to Andrew Lyon and his staff at William Collins Publishers for their help in getting this anthology published and to Bishop Robert Paterson for writing the Foreword. As always, I extend my thanks to my wife, Margaret, for her unceasing encouragement and it is to her that I dedicate this book.

ARTHUR HOWELLS

Arthur Howells is a retired Anglican priest who has served all his ministry in the Church in Wales. He is married to Margaret, a retired teacher. They live in Swansea and have two sons and four grandchildren. Formerly Canon Residentiary and Chancellor of Brecon Cathedral, he was Canon Missioner of the Diocese of Swansea and Brecon for ten years prior to his last appointment as Vicar of St James', Swansea. Since retiring in 1997 he assists in local parishes and conducts retreats and Quiet Days. A graduate of the University of Wales, Lampeter, he was awarded an MA in Celtic Christianity by the same University in 2003. He has previously compiled three Lent anthologies – A Lent Companion, Generous Love and, more recently, The Little Book of Lent.

Come, Lord, and visit us in peace
that we may rejoice before you with a perfect heart.

THE ADVENT ANTIPHON

A PRAYER BEFORE ADVENT

Lord Jesus our Saviour, the One who is to come,
we come to you now.
Our hearts are cold;
Lord, warm them by your selfless love.
Our hearts are sinful;
cleanse them with your precious blood.
Our hearts are weak;
strengthen them with your joyous Spirit.
Our hearts are empty;
fill them with your divine presence.
Come, Emmanuel:
enter our lives,
possess them always
and only
for yourself.

ST AUGUSTINE OF HIPPO (ADAPTED)

ADVENT SUNDAY

For Reflection

Sister Maria Boulding *was a contemplative nun from the Benedictine community at Stanbrook Abbey. Her books include* Marked for Life, Gateway to Hope *and* The Coming of God, *from which this extract is taken.*

Come, Lord Jesus

Every year in the weeks before Christmas the Christian Church celebrates the season called Advent, the Coming of the Lord. It is a poetic, mysterious and very beautiful time, during which the prayers and longings of the prophets and psalmists and anonymous poor people of the Old Testament come into their own. We are invited to identify with the people who waited for Christ during that long night watch, and certainly the poetic elements, combined with the darkness and stars for those who live in the north, make it easy. Nevertheless, we could be dogged by a feeling of unreality, a suspicion that there is something artificial about pretending to look forward to Christ's coming when we know that he has come already.

He has come, certainly, and that historic moment of his human birth cannot be repeated. The clock cannot be put back. The first Christmas was a gift from God which has changed human life and history, inserting into the heart of our affairs the love which gives them meaning. But the Advent we keep is not a poetic make-believe, or a nostalgic historical pageant, or even an exercise in remembering our roots, although this might have value. The coming of God in Christ still continues, and will be consummated in a coming and a gift beyond the stretch of our hope. We are an Advent people. The season of Advent celebrates in symbolic form a reality of our own lives and of all men's destiny with God, because he who came in weakness in Bethlehem is he who will come again.

Constantly he comes. He came as a man into our human situation, accepted human experience as his own and loved it through to the bitter end, in order that what was bitter might be turned into sweetness and human experience become an expression of his sacrificial, redeeming love. He has transformed it from the inside, and offered us the possibility of allowing him to transform it in our lives too. The one historical unique birth at Bethlehem makes possible his birth in the many lives of those who will receive him, to whom he gives the power to become children of God. He is born in us continually as our minds, our actions, our reactions, our relationships, our experience and our prayer are Christified. But this is a lifetime's task, and we need to pray constantly from the still pre-Christian areas in us, 'Come, Lord Jesus'...

The particular experience of the chosen people, Israel, was like a sacrament, a symbolic expression created by

God of the response and readiness that he needed in order to make his ultimate gift. In Israel the long preparation of mankind was focused. This is why we are invited to identify with Israel-the-symbol during the annual celebration of Advent. What is being expressed in this symbolic way is a reality of human life, and human life not simply for a special season of a few weeks each year, but all the time. Our lives are an Advent, a time of waiting, listening and hoping, a time of openness to the unimaginable gift of God. Israel was a focus; the Christian Church is a focus. But so are you.

THE COMING OF GOD
SISTER MARIA BOULDING

Scripture Reading

ISAIAH 55:6–11

Seek the LORD while he may be found,
    call upon him while he is near;
let the wicked forsake their way,
    and the unrighteous their thoughts;
let them return to the LORD, that he may have mercy
    on them,
    and to our God, for he will abundantly pardon.
For my thoughts are not your thoughts,
    nor are your ways my ways, says the LORD.
For as the heavens are higher than the earth,
    so are my ways higher than your ways
    and my thoughts than your thoughts.

For as the rain and snow come down from heaven,
    and do not return there until they have watered
        the earth,
making it bring forth and sprout,
    giving seed to the sower and bread to the eater,
so shall my word be that goes out from my mouth;
    it shall not return to me empty,
but it shall accomplish that which I purpose,
    and succeed in the thing for which I sent it.

Prayer

Come, Lord Jesus!
Come to us now and make your home within us.
Come to us in the people we meet,
come to us in the beauty of the world,
come to us in our joys and in our sorrows,
come to us in Word and Sacrament.
Come and make yourself known to us
in the breaking of the Word,
in the breaking of the Bread,
in the breaking of our hearts,
today, tomorrow and for ever.

MONDAY, WEEK ONE

For Reflection

Henri J. M. Nouwen (1932–96), a Dutch Catholic priest, spent twenty years teaching in the Netherlands and the USA. Through his friendship with Jean Vanier, the founder of L'Arche, he gave the last years of his life to ministering at the L'Arche Community in Toronto. In great demand as a speaker on spirituality, he was also a prolific writer. The Genesee Diary is an account of a year he spent as a contemplative in a Trappist monastery.

Waiting

'The grass withers, the flower fades, but the word of our God remains for ever' (Isaiah 40:8). The Word of God is powerful indeed. Not only the Jesus Prayer but many words from the Scriptures can reshape the inner self. When I take the words that strike me during a service into the day and slowly repeat them while reading or working, more or less chewing on them, they create new life. Sometimes when I wake up during the night I am still saying them, and they become like wings carrying me above the moods and turbulences of the days and the weeks.

In Isaiah I read: 'Young men may grow tired and weary, youths may stumble, but those who hope in Yahweh renew their strength, they put out wings like eagles. They run and do not grow weary, walk and never tire' (40:30–31). The words of God are indeed like eagles' wings. Maybe I can deepen my hope in God by giving more time and attention to his words.

Once in a while I see a monk reading from a small pocket book of the Psalms while doing something else (stirring soup, for instance). I know that he is trying to memorize the Psalms. I recently read a letter by a Trappistine sister in which she wrote that she knew more than half of the 150 psalms by heart. What a gift to be able to pray those words at any time and at any place. I can understand better now how they can give us eagles' wings and renew constantly our strength.

The words about God's coming not only remind us that God will appear, but also he will slowly transform our whole being into expectation, then all we are has become 'waiting'.

THE GENESEE DIARY
HENRI J. M. NOUWEN

Scripture Reading

ISAIAH 40:27–31

Why do you say, O Jacob,
     and speak, O Israel,
'My way is hidden from the LORD,
     and my right is disregarded by my God'?
Have you not known? Have you not heard?

The LORD is the everlasting God,
 the Creator of the ends of the earth.
He does not faint or grow weary;
 his understanding is unsearchable.
He gives power to the faint,
 and strengthens the powerless.
Even youths will faint and be weary,
 and the young will fall exhausted;
but those who wait for the LORD shall renew their
 strength,
 they shall mount up with wings like eagles,
they shall run and not be weary,
 they shall walk and not faint.

Prayer

Lord, I am poured out, I come to you for renewal.
Lord, I am weary, I come to you for refreshment.
Lord, I am worn, I come to you for restoration.
Lord, I am lost, I come to you for guidance.
Lord, I am troubled, I come to you for peace.
Lord, I am lonely, I come to you for love.
Come, Lord.
Come, revive me.
Come, re-shape me.
Come, mould me in your image.
Re-cast me in the furnace of your love.

POWER LINES
DAVID ADAM

TUESDAY, WEEK ONE

For Reflection

Father Andrew SDC (1869–1946) *was an Anglican priest who worked in the East End of London, where he co-founded the Society of Divine Compassion, the first of the Anglican religious orders for men. He was highly regarded as a spiritual guide and was also a poet, artist and writer.*

The Fullness of Time

When our Lord came to this earth in what St Paul calls 'the fullness of time', it was not only the right psychological moment, when the world was united in the great Roman empire, speaking more or less the same language, and at peace, so that travellers could travel in comparative safety. All this made it an extraordinarily good moment for the dissemination of a great gospel, but it was also the moment of the world's great need. The old pagan religions had altogether ceased to satisfy, pagan morality had become extraordinarily corrupt, and just when the world was groping in darkness and stricken with wounds, Christ came. The world needed him, and God in the Incarnation found a way to come to the world.

As we think of the present state of the world from the point of view of an ordinary man, it is not at all a hopeful situation; but, from the point of view of a Christian, we know that man's extremity is God's opportunity, and God himself will come in his own way. We are not sufficient for the situation, but God certainly is, and he will give us the power to behave in such a way as to give him glory and reveal love to our neighbour. There is no sort of guarantee that life will mechanically develop into beauty, that you and I left to ourselves will evolve into sanctity. Our hope is not in ourselves but in him. In his own hidden way he enters into our life, in the midst of our darkness, pain, and temptation. Let us not doubt that he is sufficient for our situation, that he is saving us, perhaps all unknown to ourselves, as he was the world's Saviour though the world knew him not.

MEDITATIONS FOR EVERY DAY
FATHER ANDREW SDC

Scripture Reading

GALATIANS 4:1-7
My point is this: heirs, as long as they are minors, are no better than slaves, though they are the owners of all the property; but they remain under guardians and trustees until the date set by the father. So with us; while we were minors, we were enslaved to the elemental spirits of the world. But when the fullness of time had come, God sent his son, born of a woman, born under the law, in order to redeem those who were under the law, so that we might receive adoption as children. And because you are children, God has sent the Spirit of

his Son into our hearts, crying, 'Abba! Father!' So you are no longer a slave but a child, and if a child then also an heir, through God.

Prayer

Abba! Father!
We make our cry to you now.
Look with your love and compassion
on the world which your Son came to save.
Enter our hearts, and the hearts of men and women
    everywhere
that we may be transformed, to be your people, to
    live to your glory,
to be bringers of hope and instruments of love,
sharing the joy of your Risen Life
and working for that peace which is your gift to us –
relying not on our strength but yours.

WEDNESDAY, WEEK ONE

For Reflection

Austin Farrer (1904–68), an Anglican priest, theologian and philosopher, served as Warden of Keble College, Oxford from 1960–68. Previously he was a fellow and chaplain of Trinity College, Oxford. He was the author of many theological books. The Crown of the Year is a collection of short homilies he preached at the College Chapel at the Sunday Eucharist.

God-with-us

Our journey sets out from God in our creation, and returns to God at the final judgement. As the bird rises from the earth to fly, and must some time return to the earth from which it rose; so God sends us forth to fly, and we must fall back into the hands of God at last. But God does not wait for the failure of our power and the expiry of our days to drop us back into his lap. He goes himself to meet us and everywhere confronts us. Where is the countenance which we must finally look in the eyes, and not be able to turn away our head? It smiles up at Mary from the cradle, it calls Peter from the nets, it looks on him with grief when he has denied his master. Our judge meets us at every step of our way, with forgiveness on his lips and succour in his hands.

He offers us those things while there is yet time. Every day opportunity shortens, our scope for learning our Redeemer's love is narrowed by twenty-four hours, and we come nearer to the end of our journey, when we shall fall into the hands of the living God, and touch the heart of the devouring fire...

Advent is coming, not our coming to God, but his to us. We cannot come to God, he is beyond our reach; but he can come to us, for we are not beneath his mercy. Even in another life, as St John sees it in his vision, we do not rise to God, but he descends to us, and dwells humanly among human creatures, in the glorious man, Jesus Christ. And that will be his last coming; so we shall be his people, and he everlastingly our God, our God-with-us, our Emmanuel. He will so come, but he has come already, he comes always: in our fellow-Christian (even in a child, says Christ), in his word, invisibly in our souls, more visibly in the sacrament. Opening ourselves to him, we call him in: Blessed is he that cometh in the name of the Lord; O come, Emmanuel.

THE CROWN OF THE YEAR
AUSTIN FARRER

Scripture Reading

REVELATION 21:1–7

Then I saw a new heaven and a new earth; for the first heaven and the first earth had passed away, and the sea was no more. And I saw the holy city, the new Jerusalem, coming down out of heaven from God, prepared as a bride adorned for her husband. And I heard a loud voice from the throne saying,

> 'See the home of God is among mortals.
> He will dwell with them;
> they will be his peoples,
> and God himself will be with them;
> he will wipe every tear from their eyes.
> Death will be no more;
> mourning and crying and pain will be no more,
> for the first things have passed away.'

And the one who was seated on the throne said, 'See, I am making all things new.' Also he said, 'Write this, for these words are trustworthy and true.' Then he said to me, 'It is done! I am the Alpha and Omega, the beginning and the end. To the thirsty I will give water as a gift from the spring of the water of life. Those who conquer will inherit all these things, and I will be their God and they will be my children.'

Prayer

Come, thou long-expected Jesus,
born to set thy people free;
from our fears and sins release us;
let us find our rest in thee.

Israel's strength and consolation,
hope of all the earth thou art;
dear desire of every nation,
joy of every longing heart.

Born thy people to deliver;
born a child and yet a king;
born to reign in us for ever;
now thy gracious kingdom bring.

By thy own eternal Spirit,
rule in all our hearts alone:
by thy all-sufficient merit,
raise us to thy glorious throne.

CHARLES WESLEY, 1707–88

THURSDAY,
WEEK ONE

For Reflection

Delia Smith *(b. 1941) rose to fame as a television presenter who taught the basic skills of cookery. She is a devout Roman Catholic and her* Feast for Advent *and* Feast for Lent *were bestsellers.*

The Safety of the Rock

We are instructed to build our faith on an everlasting rock. A belief that will endure suffering and hardship is one that is based on solid reality, and if we are obedient to the word of God we will eventually begin to step out in trust, understanding that this rock-like power can sustain us far beyond anything we can imagine. But to say 'Lord, Lord', to do all the right things, even to offer a lifetime of good works is not enough. What the gospel teaches us is radical commitment and radical trust: Jesus himself tells us, 'Do not worry about anything, set your hearts on the kingdom of heaven and God's righteousness first, and all that you need will be given to you as well' (Matthew 6:31–33).

I believe one of the signs of a life lived in obedience to the word of God is serenity. Serenity in a person is a sure sign of faith built on a rock of trust. And to achieve this we need to build up a relationship of real trust by learning how to trust God in the little, everyday circumstances of our lives. If you are a person who tends to worry, why not start right now? Just pray and ask the Holy Spirit to bring to mind some small anxiety that has been nagging away at you, then simply ask God to deal with it. Every time you feel it coming back to niggle you just say a short prayer: 'Into your hands, Lord, I commend such and such.' Then when you see how simply and easily God deals with it, offer thanks and take another step in trust.

A FEAST FOR ADVENT
DELIA SMITH

Scripture Reading

MATTHEW 7:24–27

'Everyone then who hears these words of mine and acts on them will be like a wise man who built his house on rock. The rain fell, the floods came, and the winds blew and beat on that house, but it did not fall, because it had been founded on rock. And everyone who hears these words of mine and does not act on them will be like a foolish man who built his house on sand. The rain fell, and the floods came, and the winds blew and beat against that house, and it fell – and great was its fall!'

PSALM 62:5-8

For God alone my soul waits in silence,
    for my hope is from him.
He alone is my rock and my salvation,
    my fortress; I shall not be shaken.
On God rests my deliverance and my honour;
    my mighty rock, my refuge is in God.

Trust in him at all times, O people;
    pour out your heart before him;
    God is a refuge for us.

Prayer

You are the rock on which I build my faith,
my trust, my hope.
You are my rock on which I build my life,
my love, my all.
You are the rock on which you build your Church,
your saints, your people.
Help us to be steadfast in our faith,
enduring in our love,
and faithful in our lives.

FRIDAY, WEEK ONE

For Reflection

Kathy Galloway *is a minister of the Church of Scotland. She is an experienced preacher, retreat conductor and broadcaster, and was formerly the leader of the Iona Community. Her books include* Love Burning Deep: Poems and Lyrics, Struggle to Love: The Spirituality of the Beatitudes *and* Imagining the Gospel. *This extract is from her book of sermons and addresses,* Getting Personal.

Keep Awake!

Advent, along with Lent, is a time of preparation. During Lent, we accompany Jesus into the desert; we face the wilderness of our own inner landscape to prepare ourselves for the Easter journey of death and resurrection. During Advent, we go with John into the desert to prepare the way to welcome Christ into our hearts and lives anew at Christmas. We have the opportunity to explore the inner geography of our lives for areas of dead wood, thorns or tangled knots. Twisted relationships, the dead wood of old hurts or habits, the confusion that sometimes comes when we feel we can't see the wood for the trees – all these are wilderness areas, and they need to be cleared away before growth and new life is possible. Or perhaps there are desert patches – arid, dry areas where nothing can grow or blossom, parts of us which have withered away from not being used or tended or tested – some tenderness, some care, some talent, some forgiveness, some humour that need the water of life to bring them bursting into flower.

If we have desert or wilderness places within us – and which of us do not? – Advent is a good time to prepare for new life, for the birth of Christ within us, to clear the way so that we have more courageous self-examination, more open hearts, more receptive spirits, more loving kindness towards ourselves and others. We don't and can't know what that will mean for us, and it will probably not be what we expect, but when that call to worship, to accept, and to walk the road of love comes again with renewed vigour, we want to be prepared, to be ready.

So, a word of preparation, sometimes dramatic, sometimes quiet and steady. And the first necessity for our walking the way of love is that we should be on our feet. 'Rise from the dust, undo the chains that bind you', says Isaiah. 'Be awake and sober', says Jesus. We can't walk sitting down, far less crumpled in a heap. To stand up very often means to stand out, and to stand up for the way of love is not, it seems, a very acceptable stance at the moment. Nevertheless, by grace it is both our calling and our charism, our gift, our freedom. Let us encourage and support one another to embrace our calling and our freedom this Advent.

GETTING PERSONAL
KATHY GALLOWAY

Scripture Reading

1 THESSALONIANS 5:1–11

Now concerning the times and the seasons, brothers and sisters, you do not need to have anything written to you. For you yourselves know very well that the day of the Lord will come like a thief in the night. When they say, 'There is peace and security', then sudden destruction will come upon them, as labour pains come upon a pregnant woman, and there will be no escape! But you, beloved, are not in darkness, for that day to surprise you like a thief; for you are all children of light and children of the day; we are not of the night or of darkness. So then, let us not fall asleep as others do, but let us keep awake and be sober; for those who sleep, sleep at night, and those who are drunk get drunk at night. But since we belong to the day, let us be sober, and put on the breastplate of faith and love, and for a helmet the hope of salvation. For God has destined us not for wrath but for obtaining salvation through our Lord Jesus Christ, who died for us, so that whether we are awake or asleep we may live with him. Therefore encourage one another and build up each other, as indeed you are doing.

Prayer

Love translated in the Lord Jesus – give us that love.
Love in our thinking,
love in our speaking,
love in all that we do;
love to our dear ones,
love to our friends,
love to our neighbours.

Love to those we find difficult,
love in joy, love in sorrow.
Awaken within us that love which comes from you.
Raise us up to walk the path of love in your
 company,
today, tomorrow and always.

SATURDAY, WEEK ONE

For Reflection

Michael Stancliffe (1916–87) *was ordained to the Anglican priesthood in 1940. He was chaplain of Westminster School before his appointment as a canon of Westminster Abbey and Rector of St Margaret's, Westminster. In 1961 he was appointed chaplain to the Speaker of the House of Commons. Eight years later he became Dean of Winchester. With a gift for words and images, he contributed a regular religious column in the* Daily Telegraph.

Be Still

Elijah came to Horeb where he found faith and courage in the Lord. And where did he find the Lord? Not, we are told, in the roaring of the wind, nor in the commotion and convulsion of the earthquake, nor in the terrible power of the fire – but in a still, small voice. He had reached the still point at the centre.

Eight centuries later God himself came down from heaven and through taking flesh entered the revolving stream of change and decay and lived in the midst of giddy twisting humans. And one of his most telling characteristics was his stillness. In Jesus, busy and giddy and demented people found peace and repose. 'Come unto me, all that travail and are heavy laden, and I will refresh you,' he invited them. So Mary came and sat at his feet and was still, and busy Martha was urged to do likewise. Lunatics were found sitting at his feet, composed and in their right minds. And the words that he spoke were neither clever chat nor idle gossip, neither vulgar boasting nor loud opinion; such words as he spoke were recognized as words of love, of truth, and of no ordinary power and authority. Experienced boatmen panicked around him, but Jesus had merely to say to the elements, 'Peace, be still,' and there was a great calm. Even when the wildest cyclone of human sin and demonic evil broke upon him, his stillness remained. Cross-examined by men bent upon his destruction, he held his peace – he held his peace. Nailed to the cross, he remained unmoved while men made circles round him and taunted him to prove his divinity by coming down from the cross. Being the person he was, he stayed where he was – at the still centre; and, as many of those who have not called themselves Christians have recognized since, he mastered that scene on the green hill and was not mastered by it.

For the still centre is the source of all life and power and might ... 'Be still and know that I am God' (Psalm 46:10): so we are commanded, as the winds and waves of the Sea of Galilee were commanded. We are to be still because, by that means, we may come closest to God, to the core and centre of all things. We are to be still because, by that means, we may sit at his feet, clothed and in our right minds and able to hear the still small voice. We are to be still because, by that means, we may be delivered from dizziness and business and may find both the peace that passes understanding and the source of all power and might. 'Be still and know that I am God'.

STARS AND ANGELS
MICHAEL STANCLIFFE

Scripture Reading

1 KINGS 19:9–13

At that place he came to a cave, and spent the night there.

Then the word of the LORD came to him, saying, 'What are you doing here, Elijah?' He answered, 'I have been very zealous for the LORD, the God of hosts; for the Israelites have forsaken your covenant, thrown down your altars, and killed your prophets with the sword. I alone am left, and they are seeking my life, to take it away.'

He said, 'Go out and stand on the mountain before the LORD, for the LORD is about to pass by.' Now there was a great wind, so strong that it was splitting mountains and breaking rocks in pieces before the LORD, but the LORD was not in the wind; and after the wind an earthquake, but the LORD was not in the earthquake; and after the earthquake, a fire, but the LORD was not in the fire; and after the fire the sound of sheer silence. When Elijah heard it, he wrapped his face in his mantle and went out and stood at the entrance to the cave.

Prayer

Lord, teach me to be still,
when I am disturbed, distressed, disgusted,
when I am angry, troubled, tempted.

Lord, teach me to be still,
in disappointment, pain, sorrow.

As I enter into your presence
in stillness and silence,
may I hear your voice
and respond to your call.

THE SECOND SUNDAY
IN ADVENT

For Reflection

Trystan Owain Hughes (b. 1972), *a Christian theologian and historian, was chaplain at Cardiff University before his appointment as priest in charge of Christ Church, Cardiff. The author of a variety of theological publications, he is also a regular contributor to BBC Radio 2's* Pause for Thought *and Radio 4's* Prayer for the Day.

Job's Comforters

When we pity we often act as if we know better than the other person, while compassion simply leads us to feel the suffering of another as if it were our own – we willingly enter the places of pain in people's lives.

In the Old Testament, Job's friends are initially inspired towards compassion, as they go to him with the aim of standing alongside and comforting their distraught friend. On arriving, they empathize with his lot by entering his suffering in a way typical of Israelite culture – by weeping, tearing their clothing and throwing dust on themselves. They then sit with Job in silence for a whole week, 'because they saw how great his suffering was' (Job 2:13). Their very presence was their compassion. If that had been the conclusion of the story, it might indeed be an ideal model of incarnational compassion, albeit one rooted in the cultural practices of the ancient Near East. Unfortunately for the next 35 chapters these friends ruin their earlier work by offering empty, critical and patronizing opinions on Job's predicament. Too often we are drawn to offer advice or counsel when we see someone suffering. Compassion, however, simply calls us to be there for those in need. I have a small box at home that is stuffed with scribbled notes and business cards I have acquired since my diagnosis of a degenerative spinal condition, containing the names of osteopaths, physiotherapists, chiropractors, acupuncturists, and Reiki specialists. They have been given to me by friends, colleagues, and even strangers on trains who notice that I have to get up and walk around the carriage at every opportunity. Certainly all these people had a real desire to bring relief to my pain and, as such, their gestures were kindly and loving. Yet too often many of us fail to recognize that mere kindness is not enough and those suffering need something very different from 'advice'. The aspiration to 'mend' or to 'cure' is clearly well-meaning, but the real need of people who are suffering is an incarnational and compassionate giving of time and attention.

The road to compassion, however, will rarely offer us a smooth path ... By being compassionate we engage in real life, and real life naturally involves risks and dangers, including ingratitude. Thus compassion will often ask of us a marked personal sacrifice.

Standing alongside those who suffer is part of the costly discipleship championed by Dietrich Bonhoeffer. By its very nature, such discipleship makes demands on us, as we embrace the crucifixion by following the way of the cross. Yet compassion should never be masochistic. St Paul continually relates compassionate service to both sacrifice and joy, reminding us that while compassion is not always easy, it can still be acted on with a sense of hope and joy.

THE COMPASSIONATE QUEST
TRYSTAN OWAIN HUGHES

Scripture Reading

JOB 2:11-13

Now when Job's three friends heard of all these troubles that had come upon him, each of them set out from his home – Eliphaz the Temanite, Bildad the Shuhite, and Zophar the Naamathite. They met together to go and console and comfort him. When they saw him from a distance, they did not recognize him, and they raised their voices and wept aloud; they tore their robes and threw dust in the air upon their heads. They sat with him on the ground for seven days and seven nights, and no one spoke a word to him, for they saw that his suffering was very great.

Prayer

Lord Jesus, I give you my hands to do your work;
I give you my feet to go your way;
I give you my eyes to see as you do.

I give you my tongue to speak your words;
I give you my mind, Lord, that you may think in me;
I give you my spirit that you may pray in me.

Above all, Lord, I give you my heart,
that you may love in me your Father and all
    humankind;
I give you my whole self that you may grow in me,
so that it is you, Lord Jesus,
who live and work and pray in me.

Lord Jesus, I give you my spirit that you may pray
    in me;
I give you my heart, Lord,
that you may love in me.

THE GRAIL PRAYER

MONDAY, WEEK TWO

For Reflection

David Adam (b. 1936), *until his retirement, was Vicar of Holy Island, Lindisfarne, where his work involved ministry to thousands of pilgrims and visitors. He has published several books of prayers composed in the Celtic pattern, including* The Edge of Glory, The Cry of the Deer, The Open Gate, Power Lines *and* Tides and Seasons.

God Is Near You

The prophet Isaiah, seeking to encourage his people and offering them strength for the new freedom that is being held out to them. Many of these people had been born into captivity and did not know what freedom was. They had dreamed of returning to their homeland, but in reality a good few would rather not make the perilous journey. They had food and security where they were and were now being asked to venture into the unknown. Were they strong enough to travel? Were they willing to sacrifice the present comfort for the desert and the difficulties that lay ahead? It was the prophet's task to offer them the strength of their God and his calling to his people. This was like the Exodus all over again. Freed from captivity, they would be marching to the Promised Land. This was not a simple journey, there was the river

Euphrates to cross and, beyond that, the desert. The prophet, like all prophets, declares to the people: 'God is with you; you are not going in your own strength but in the strength of God. As God was with the children of Israel at the waters of the Red Sea, he will be with you. As he was with Moses in the burning heat of the Negeb desert he will be with you. Do not be afraid, for the Lord is with you. God has chosen you.' As ever, God is calling and the people are stalling ... They are asked to see that they are not going in their own strength, but in the power and presence of God. Do not fear, God is near!

God is with you today as you venture into the unknown, God is with you in your joys and in your sorrows. You are not alone in your journey. You are not forsaken in trial or tribulation, for God is ever with you. How often have you failed to venture because you felt alone and called to act in your strength alone? Know that you are not alone and God is calling you to a more wonderful freedom and life than you ever dreamed of. You are not only called by God, he knows you and your needs. He will bring his strength to your weakness, and dispel your fear with his presence.

Know that God wants us to seek newness in his world, to discover new insights and to learn new things. God speaks to us through the discoveries that are made, as they help us to extend our way of thinking and not live with a closed-circuit mind. We should seek to discover something new each day and to give thanks to God for it.

CANDLES IN THE DARK
DAVID ADAM

Scripture Reading

ISAIAH 43:1-5a

But now thus says the LORD,
he who created you, O Jacob,
   he who formed you, O Israel:
Do not fear, for I have redeemed you;
   I have called you by name, you are mine.
When you pass through the waters, I will be with you;
   and through the rivers, they shall not overwhelm
      you;
when you walk through fire you shall not be burned,
   and the flame shall not consume you.
For I am the Lord your God,
   the Holy One of Israel, your Saviour.
I give Egypt as your ransom,
   Ethiopia and Seba in exchange for you.
Because you are precious in my sight,
   and honoured, and I love you,
I give people in return for you,
   nations in exchange for your life.
Do not fear, for I am with you.

Prayer

Blessed are you, Lord God of all creation,
you make light to shine in the darkness.
You guided the children of Israel and led them,
after many trials and tribulations,
to the Promised Land.
As you called them so you call us.
We ask you to give us strength in our weakness,
to dispel our fear of the unknown,
to help us to know that we walk in your light
and that you are always near us,
leading us to freedom as your children.

TUESDAY, WEEK TWO

For Reflection

The Gift of Peace

If you are to be able to respond to the invitation in prayer, 'Be still', you need a measure of silence in your life. In today's world silence is in short supply; this is a serious problem for our society, and anything we can do to help people recover a sense of silence as a necessary and positive element in human life is a contribution to the general sanity. Many people can, however, contrive some islands of silence in their lives, perhaps in holiday time. Without romantically ignoring our dependence on our environment, it is also true to say that silence is partly an interior quality; you can learn to live from your own deep centre, rather than in the ego with its clamorous demands. You can make positive use of any period of silence that does occur, rather than looking on it as an empty stretch of time to be endured or filled up somehow. Silence like this is not a threat to us but an invitation to depth, to listening, to a loving communion in joy. It lays us open to the strong creativity of the Spirit, and he is the Spirit both of contemplation and outgoing love. Contemplation, trust and reaching out to people go together. Mary's silent surrender to God at the

Annunciation sent her swiftly out in the generous and practical love of the Visitation. Christ is in you, yours to give, a quiet light.

It may help us, when we are painfully conscious of turmoil, to remember that Christ's gifts are more than a spiritualized version of secular commodities. As the love he gives us is a love that has made itself vulnerable to all that hatred can do and has conquered hatred, as the life he gives is a life that has been given through death and proved the stronger, so the peace he gives is something more than an absence of stress: 'Peace I leave with you; my peace I give to you; not as the world gives do I give to you' (John 14:27). The gift may sometimes be offered and received within the turmoil, in the eye of the storm.

THE COMING OF GOD
SISTER MARIA BOULDING

Scripture Reading

JOHN 14:25–31

I have said these things to you while I am still with you. But the Advocate, the Holy Spirit, whom the Father will send in my name, will teach you everything, and remind you of all that I have said to you. Peace I leave with you; my peace I give to you. I do not give to you as the world gives. Do not let your hearts be troubled, and do not let them be afraid. You heard me say to you, 'I am going away, and I am coming to you.' If you loved me you would rejoice that I am going to the Father, because the Father is greater than I. And now I have told you this before it occurs, so that when it does occur, you may believe. I will no longer talk much with you, for the ruler of this world is coming. He has no power over me; but I do as the Father commanded me, so that the world may know that I love the Father.

Prayer

Lord Jesus –
in my restlessness may I find rest in you.
In my fears may I find peace with you.
In my confusion may I find understanding in you.
In my wanderings may I find my true home in you.

WEDNESDAY, WEEK TWO

For Reflection

Timothy Radcliffe OP (b. 1945) is a Dominican friar. Educated at Oxford and Paris, he taught theology at Oxford and was involved in a ministry to people with AIDS. He is the author of Sing a New Song, I Call You Friends, Why Go to Church? *and* What is the Point of Being a Christian? *This quotation is from his book,* Take the Plunge.

Pilgrim People

The Israelites crossed the Red Sea and set off into the wilderness, hoping eventually to arrive at the Promised Land. The Israelites took a long time arriving at their destination. On the way they bickered, succumbed to idolatry, were tempted to go back to the onions and cucumbers and garlic of Egypt and to slavery, demanded meat and got angry with their leaders. Finally when they got to its borders and saw that its inhabitants were tall and strong, most of them lost their nerve.

In the Letter to the Hebrews, we are seen to be like them, travelling in the wilderness, waiting to enter the Promised Land which is God's own rest. The Church remains much like the people of Israel in the Sinai desert. We seem to be going around in circles, bickering, demanding strong leadership and then rejecting it if we get it. We too suffer from crises of confidence and faith, fear that God has forgotten us, and may even be tempted to give up the whole adventure and settle for whatever Egypt has to offer us. So the newly baptized have not joined a triumphant group. Jean Vanier said we advance more like rabbits sniffing our way forward than like giraffes who can see the way ahead (Vanier, *Essential Writings*).

Pilgrims cannot be weighed down by much baggage. We shall have to shed much of it if we are to travel, beginning with images of God. Eckhart said, 'If you think of anything He might be He is not that.' (Woods: *Meister Eckhart*, p. 86). We may have to let go of images of the Church. It does not turn out to be the community of radiant charity that we hoped for, but a crowd of unimpressive people who are often unsure and afraid, inclined to make shameful compromises and do not dare to tell their doubts and questions truthfully. God's holy people do not seem so holy after all. But this stripping away of illusions is also part of our journey to the Promised Land and we must give each other courage for the way...

In 1833 the young John Henry Newman was becalmed off the coast of Sardinia. He was depressed, exhausted and could not see his way forward. And so, with nothing else to do he composed poems, most famously the hymn 'Lead, kindly light':

Lead, kindly light, amid th'encircling gloom,
lead thou me on;
the night is dark, and I am far from home;
lead thou me on.
Keep thou my feet; I do not ask to see
the distant scene; one step enough for me.

So we are baptized as pilgrims on the way to the Kingdom. For this we need courage. In the baptism of children, after the Our Father, the parents, godparents and the whole congregation are blessed. The child is at the beginning of the journey, and may well have to struggle with doubts, tough questions, may wander all over the place, like those Israelites in the desert, and so we are blessed that we may give him or her and each of us the courage as we travel, unafraid of anything: 'May God watch over your life, and may we all walk by the light of faith and attain the good things he has promised us.'

TAKE THE PLUNGE
TIMOTHY RADCLIFFE OP

Scripture Reading

PSALM 121

> I lift up my eyes to the hills –
>> from where will my help come?
> My help comes from the LORD,
>> who made heaven and earth.
>
> He will not let your foot be moved;
>> he who keeps you will not slumber.
> He who keeps Israel
>> will neither slumber nor sleep.
>
> The LORD is your keeper;
>> the LORD is your shade at your right hand.
> The sun shall not strike you by day,
>> nor the moon by night.
>
> The LORD will keep you from all evil;
>> he will keep your life.
> The LORD will keep
>> your going out and your coming in
>> from this time on and for evermore.

Prayer

You are the object of our journey.
You are the One who leads us onward.
You are the Light in the gloom.
You are the Forgiving One.
You are the Peace Giver.
You are the Accompanier.
You are the Incarnate One.
Come to guide us,
to lead us
and forgive us.
Glory be to you, my God and King.

THURSDAY,
WEEK TWO

For Reflection

Launch Out

See the fishermen mending their nets. Look at the weariness upon them. They are on the beach, and their boats are beached also. It is as if the tide has left them all behind. Their nets have broken and they have taken them into their hands. Great holes that let life slip through have to be repaired. At the moment it seems that life is escaping from them, slipping through the net and through their fingers. They know it is necessary to make the holes smaller. If the mesh is too large, everything will escape them, so they are mending their nets.

It is at such a moment that he comes. He comes when life seems to be escaping us. He comes when we toil all night and get nothing for it. Beware, he is wanting to cast his net and he is making the casting area smaller. He does not want everyone just to slip away. See him being jostled by the crowds. The beach is becoming so crowded, he can hardly move. If he is to land a great catch like this he will need help. So he calls to the fishermen. He wants their support. He needs a little space. So he borrows their boat – and the fishermen. For a while the talking goes on but then Jesus comes to the important bit: 'Thrust out a little from the land' – a simple request, but it is the beginning of something bigger. It is nice being there with the gentle movement of the boat. They begin to wonder why they do not do this more often. It is so relaxing, so refreshing. Because of this action they feel especially close to Him. He is in their boat – and in their lives.

'Launch out into the deep!' That order comes as a bit of a shock. It seems that privileges always bring with them responsibilities. They were just beginning to lie back. 'Launch into the deep!' He wants them to be in the deep waters. He knows that big catches are not in these shallows. 'Launch out into the deep and let down your nets for a catch.' Peter wanted to object but he also wanted to plumb new depths, so he obeyed. Here was a catch like never before; though the fishermen were not quite sure who was catching what or whom. All Peter knew was that they had entered the deep with Jesus and their lives would never be the same again. Peter knew that when they came down to earth, when they came to land, they were caught. See what new depths they enter as they leave all behind and follow him.

Begin to learn 'the glorious liberty of the children of God'. Move out from the crowd and noise each day, so that you may know he is in your boat, your house, your life. If you do not do this, you are hardly ready for the next call, 'Launch out into the deep.' Learn to live in the deep, with a deeper awareness of the world, your neighbour and your God.

TIDES AND SEASONS
DAVID ADAM

Scripture Reading

LUKE 5:1-11

Once while Jesus was standing beside the lake of Gennesaret, and the crowd was pressing in on him to hear the word of God, he saw two boats there at the shore of the lake; the fishermen had gone out of them and were washing their nets. He got into one of the boats, the one belonging to Simon, and asked him to put out a little way from the shore. Then he sat down and taught the crowds from the boat. When he had finished speaking, he said to Simon, 'Put out into deep water and let down your nets for a catch.' [in the King James Version: 'Launch out into the deep']. Simon answered, 'Master, we have worked all night long but have caught nothing. Yet if you say so, I will let down the nets.' When they had done this, they caught so many fish that their nets were beginning to break. So they signalled to their partners in the other boat to come and help them. And they came and filled both boats, so that they began to sink. But when Simon Peter saw it, he fell down at Jesus' knees saying, 'Go away from me, Lord, for I am a sinful man!' For he and all who were with him were amazed at the catch of fish that they had taken; and so also were James and John, sons of Zebedee, who were partners with Simon. Then Jesus said to Simon, 'Do not be afraid; from now on you will be catching people.' When they had brought their boats to shore, they left everything and followed him.

Prayer

While we are doing routine work, he comes.

While we are mending our nets or our cars, he
comes.

While the very life we seek is slipping through our
fingers, he comes.

When we toil all night and catch nothing, he comes.

When we are tired and frustrated, he comes.

And every time he comes, he calls.

He calls us today and every day.

'Thrust out from the land.' Do not be earth bound
or desk bound.

TIDES AND SEASONS
DAVID ADAM

FRIDAY, WEEK TWO

For Reflection

Rowan Williams (b. 1950), is a distinguished theologian, writer and poet, and a former Archbishop of Canterbury. Since 2013 he has been Master of Magdalene College, Cambridge. He is the author of countless theological works and articles. This extract is from Being Christian, a series of Holy Week addresses he gave at Canterbury Cathedral.

The Welcome

There are many stories about Jesus and hospitality in the Gospels, but there is one in particular that tell us something very crucial about the Eucharist. It is the story in Luke 19 of Jesus' arrival in Jericho and his meeting with Zacchaeus. Zacchaeus the tax collector is worried that he will be unable to see over the heads in the crowd, so he climbs a tree, hoping that nobody will notice. Jesus stops underneath the tree and looks up. You can imagine several thousand pairs of eyes looking up at the same moment towards a scarlet faced tax collector perched on a branch – and the collective intake of breath when Jesus says to him, 'Aren't you going to ask me to your home?'

In other words Jesus is not someone who exercises hospitality; he draws out hospitality from others. By his welcome he makes other people capable of welcoming.

And the wonderful alternation in the Gospels between Jesus giving hospitality and receiving hospitality shows us something absolutely essential about the Eucharist. We are the guests of Jesus. We are there because he asks us, and because he wants our company. At the same time we are set free to invite Jesus into our lives and literally to receive him into our bodies in the Eucharist. His welcome gives us the courage to open up to him. And so the flow of giving and receiving, of welcome and acceptance, moves backwards and forwards without a break. We are welcomed and we welcome; we welcome God and we welcome our unexpected neighbours. That, surely, is one of the wonderful and unique things about the Holy Eucharist. We invoke Jesus and his Spirit, we call him to be present – and we are able to do this only because he has first called us to be present. His way of welcoming Zacchaeus, and his way of welcoming us, is to say, 'Aren't you going to ask me to your home?'

The giving and receiving of welcome is central to the way in which Jesus' ministry is portrayed in the Gospels. But it is not just an agreeable personal habit that Jesus has, and it is not a decorative addition to the main business of his ministry, a sort of pleasant extra. It is the actual, visible way in which he engages in remaking a community. Who are the real people of God now? The ones who accept Jesus' invitation. Not the ones who fulfil all the cultic demands, not the ones who score highly on the scale of piety, but the ones who are willing to hear him say, 'Aren't you going to ask me home?' It is as simple as that. The meals that Jesus shares in his ministry are the way in which he begins to re-create a community, to lay the foundations for rethinking what the words 'the people of God' mean.

BEING CHRISTIAN
ROWAN WILLIAMS

Scripture Reading

LUKE 19:1–10

He entered Jericho and was passing through it. A man was there named Zacchaeus; he was a chief tax-collector and was rich. He was trying to see who Jesus was, but on account of the crowd he could not, because he was short in stature. So he ran ahead and climbed a sycamore tree to see him, because he was going to pass that way. When Jesus came to the place, he looked up and said to him, 'Zacchaeus, hurry and come down; for I must stay in your house today.' So he hurried down and was happy to welcome him. All who saw it began to grumble and said, 'He has gone to be the guest of one who is a sinner.' Zacchaeus stood there and said to the Lord, 'Look, half of my possessions, Lord, I will give to the poor; and if I have defrauded anyone of anything I will pay back four times as much.' Then Jesus said to him, 'Today salvation has come to this house, because he too is a son of Abraham. For the Son of Man came to seek out and save the lost.'

Prayer

Lord Jesus, Host and Guest,
you valued Zacchaeus and shared a meal with him.
So we come to you –
not worthy to receive you
but knowing that you come to us
and value us
and welcome us. Shape us to be your people –
that adoring you by faith
we may in joy receive you
and with love and thanksgiving abide in you,
our Guide, the Bread of pilgrims,
our Friend and Companion along the Way.

SATURDAY,
WEEK TWO

For Reflection

Andrew Jones (b. 1961) is Archdeacon of Meirionydd and rector of four parishes on the Lleyn Peninsular. He regularly leads pilgrimages and is the author of Every Pilgrim's Guide to Celtic Britain and Ireland.

One Foot in the Kingdom

It is in this weaving of our life with God's life that we are able to discover our proper identity as human beings. lrenaeus of Lyons, one of the first great theologians of the Western church, once said that the true glory of God is to be seen in men and women living life authentically and to the full, and that authentic life is the true vision of God. By living with a pilgrim consciousness – recognizing that God is our beginning and our end, and that the physical journey of human living is a pilgrimage from God, which will ultimately take us back to God – we can begin to understand why we were created, the reason for our very being. In this way, the pilgrim can come to recognize that all of life is constantly flowing towards the presence of God, towards an end that really has no end. Pilgrimage is ultimately about progressing into the heart of God. It is about journeying together into God's call to perfection and into a fullness of life that can only, because of the very nature of its being by God's own generous invitation, constantly grow as a deep response to divine grace.

The fast and greedy pace of the world will always stand in the way of this process of spiritual maturing. To grow in faith and hope cannot, by definition of the age we live in, happen naturally. It cannot and never will happen when people insist on moving at a pace that is out of sync with their souls. Again and again I have seen how pilgrimage encourages people to slow down, turn towards God and recognize in him an infinite source of faithfulness, hope and love – the signs of true covenant. All too often, though, this kind of measured and authentic living is threatened by people's becoming less trusting of others, less committed to relationships, less hopeful about the future, more pessimistic about matters of faith and far more cynical about the very existence of God. Only by being rooted and grounded in the story of God's creative and redeeming work will we find growth and renewal of faith. Unless pilgrims know at least some of the story before they begin their journey, they will struggle to understand the story fully – and themselves in relation to the story – when they arrive at their destination...

In the depths of God's grace, we know that the gift of true gospel living is embracing the knowledge that we already live as part of God's kingdom here and now. All the Gospels show us that as a covenant people, we already have one foot in the kingdom and are able to participate here on earth the joys of heaven. But none of this is strictly our own, to be kept as private property; rather, it is a gift to be shared. For it is only when the gift of grace is truly recognized, celebrated and shared that it can offer life and nourishment to our arid and starving world – and to our tired Church that is nevertheless eternally beloved of God.

PILGRIMAGE
ANDREW JONES

Scripture Reading

HEBREWS 11:8-10, 13-16

By faith Abraham obeyed when he was called to set out for a place that he was to receive as an inheritance; and he set out, not knowing where he was going. By faith he stayed for a time in the land he had been promised, as in a foreign land, living in tents, as did Isaac and Jacob, who were heirs with him of the same promise. For he looked forward to the city that has foundations, whose architect and builder is God ... All of these died in faith without having received the promises, but from a distance they saw and greeted them. They confessed that they were strangers and foreigners on the earth, for people who speak in this way make it clear that they are seeking a homeland. If they had been thinking of the land that they had left behind, they would have had opportunity to return. But as it is, they desire a better country, that is, a heavenly one. Therefore God is not ashamed to be called their God; indeed, he has prepared a city for them.

Prayer

God of patriarchs, prophets, saints and sinners –
the beginning and the end of our pilgrimage.
Be with us on our journey.
Guide us in times of trial,
give us gladness in sorrow,
your presence in our loneliness
and fill our lives with the light of Christ
as we rejoice in fellowship
with you and all your people.

THE THIRD SUNDAY
IN ADVENT

For Reflection

Have Patience!

Cardinal Newman said that 'the Christian is the one who watches for Christ'. The whole liturgical year forms us to be a people with the courage to wait until the Lord comes. Advent trains us in the patience not to begin celebrating too early, resisting the temptation to celebrate Christ's birth before he comes although the shops are filled with signs saying 'Merry Christmas', fighting the impulse to open the presents before Christmas Day. Christ is a gift and one respects the gift by waiting for the moment when it is given. This waiting is not mere passivity. The Latin word for 'to wait', *attendere*, means to stretch oneself forward. We are attentive, opening ourselves to what will come, like a mother preparing to give birth. The whole year is marked by moments of waiting: Holy Saturday makes us pause between death and resurrection and wait for the moment of triumph, just as we wait between Ascension and Pentecost for the gift of the Holy Spirit. The Christian year forms us in patience.

Why is our waiting so much part of being a Christian? Why cannot God give us now what we long for, justice for the poor and perfect happiness for us all? Almost 2,000 years have passed since the resurrection and still we wait for the Kingdom. Why? One reason why our God takes so much time is because he is not a god. Our God is not a powerful celestial superman, a sort of invisible President Bush on a cosmic scale who might come bursting in from the outside. The coming of God is not like the cavalry cantering in to our rescue. God comes from within, inside our deepest interiority. He is, as St Augustine said, closer to us than we are to ourselves or, as the Qur'an says, closer to us than our jugular vein.

...During Advent, we are like people gathered around the bed; we await the birth. But God's coming was not just the birth of a child; it was the coming of a word. One might say that it was the coming of a language. It needed hundreds of years for English to evolve to the point at which Shakespeare might write *Hamlet*. The language had to be formed by innumerable men and women, poets and lawyers, preachers and philosophers, before it was ready for his creativity. English society had to undergo a profound transformation before the English language could be fertilized by Shakespeare's creativity.

In a similar way it needed thousands of years before there was a language in which God's word could be spoken in the form of Jesus ... The Word of God does not come down from heaven like a celestial Esperanto: it wells up within human language. The birth pangs of

the Word started when the first human beings began
to speak.

WHAT IS THE POINT OF BEING A CHRISTIAN?
TIMOTHY RADCLIFFE OP

Scripture Reading

ROMANS 8:22–27

We know that the whole creation has been groaning in
labour pains until now; and not only the creation, but
we ourselves, who have the first fruits of the Spirit, groan
inwardly while we wait for adoption, the redemption of
our bodies. For in hope we were saved. Now hope that
is seen is not hope. For who hopes for what is seen?
But if we hope for what we do not see, we wait for it
with patience.

Likewise the Spirit helps us in our weakness; for we
do not know how to pray as we ought, but that very
Spirit intercedes with sighs too deep for words. And
God, who searches the heart, knows what is the mind
of the Spirit, because the Spirit intercedes for the saints
according to the will of God.

Prayer

Lord, as we prepare for your coming at Bethlehem
we watch with patience.
As the Word became flesh and lived and moved
    among us,
so we search for you,
that in finding you we may respond with hearts
    and minds
to that Love, born of Mary; to the Word made flesh,
    dwelling in us,
so that we may dwell in him.

MONDAY, WEEK THREE

For Reflection

Stephen Rand *is a writer and speaker. Co-chair of the Jubilee Debt Campaign, he was among those responsible for the Make Poverty History Campaign in 2005. He and his wife lead a Baptist Church in Wimbledon.*

Zechariah

Zechariah was prostrate before God, and from this position he heard that God's impact on his life was not to be held within the walls of the Temple. He and Elizabeth were to be granted their greatest wish: a son. He reacted with understandable amazement – and was rendered speechless. It meant a dramatic end to a dramatic moment. Zechariah was supposed to come out from the Holy Place to reassure the people that he had not been struck dead in God's presence, and then pronounce Aaron's high-priestly blessing over the people. The delay made the people nervous; then there was relief when he appeared, followed by the realization that something significant had happened, which had left him speechless.

He wasn't speechless when John the Baptist was born, though. Zechariah had been patient for nine months. Now worship, thankfulness and praise poured out. It was not an uncommon reaction for new fathers – and this was a father who knew that God had intervened miraculously and generously in his life. As Luke tells us:

> Zechariah was filled with the Holy Spirit and prophesied:
>
> 'Praise be to the Lord, the God of Israel, because he has come and has redeemed his people. He has raised up a horn of salvation for us in the house of his servant David (as he said through his holy prophets of long ago), salvation from our enemies and from the hand of all who hate us – to show mercy to our fathers and to remember his holy covenant, the oath he swore to our father Abraham: to rescue us from the hand of our enemies, and to enable us to serve him without fear in holiness and righteousness before him all our days.
>
> 'And you, my child, will be called a prophet of the Most High; for you will go before the Lord to prepare a way for him, to give his people the knowledge of salvation through the forgiveness of their sins, because of the tender mercy of our God, by which the rising sun will come to us from heaven to shine on those living in darkness and in the shadow of death, to guide our feet into the path of peace.'
>
> LUKE 1:67–79

Zechariah rejoiced not just because God had kept his promise to him, but because he recognized that the promises of God to his people from long ago were now being fulfilled. This was not a parochial prayer focused on himself; this was a big-picture prayer, a paean of praise to God for his redemption, his salvation, his promise-keeping, his forgiveness. It was about a new life in place of death, the coming of peace...

We need to encourage one another by recognizing God's goodness to us, to his whole creation. Zechariah would never forget the day he met with God; he would never forget to be thankful for all that God had done in his history and the history of his people – and neither should we.

WHEN THE TIME WAS RIGHT
STEPHEN RAND

Scripture Reading

LUKE 1:10-20

Now at the time of incense-offering, the whole assembly of people was praying outside. Then there appeared to him an angel of the Lord, standing at the right side of the altar of incense. When Zechariah saw him, he was terrified; and fear overwhelmed him. But the angel said to him, 'Do not be afraid, Zechariah, for your prayer has been heard. Your wife Elizabeth will bear you a son, and you will name him John. You will have joy and gladness, and many will rejoice at his birth, for he will be great in the sight of the Lord. He must never drink wine or strong drink; even before his birth he will be filled with the Holy Spirit. He will turn many of the people of Israel to the Lord their God. With the spirit and power of Elijah he will go before him, to turn the hearts of parents to their children, and the disobedient to the wisdom of the righteous, to make ready a people prepared for the Lord.' Zechariah said to the angel, 'How will I know that this is so? For I am an old man, and my wife is getting on in years.' The angel replied, 'I am Gabriel. I stand in the presence of God, and I have been sent to speak to you and to bring you this good news. But now, because you did not believe my words, which will be fulfilled in their time, you will become mute, unable to speak, until the day these things occur.'

Prayer

Blessed are you, Lord God
for raising up your servants
Zechariah and Elizabeth,
Mary and Joseph,
to prepare the way for Jesus.
Blessed are you for coming to us.
We rejoice as you enter into this world with peace
    and love
and turn our darkness into the light of your presence.

TUESDAY,
WEEK THREE

For Reflection

Donald Coggan (1909–2000) *was the 101st Archbishop of Canterbury. He had a distinguished ministry, beginning as curate of Islington. He became Bishop of Bradford in 1956, Archbishop of York in 1961 and succeeded Michael Ramsay at Canterbury in 1974. As well as writing several theological books he was a regular contributor to* Theology.

Servant-Mother

Mary's reply is more powerful for its superb simplicity: 'I am the Lord's servant; may it be as you have said.'

'The Lord's servant.' Here is Mary as Servant-Mother. Hold on to that reply and ponder it. For it may be that it gives us a clue – the clue? – to the meaning of her son's life and death. The Servant-Mother was about to bear him who, above all others, was to be the servant of the Lord.

Who knows the influence of a mother on her unborn child? Here is a world of mystery which is still not wholly understood. But is it not possible that something of the concept of dedicated servanthood which was at the very heart of this young pregnant woman 'got through' to the child as yet unborn, and became an integral part in the shaping of his manhood and his ministry? There may be more in this than has been generally recognized.

Be that as it may, of this we may be certain. Mary saw, with a God-given clarity, at the moment of her greatest crisis, that servanthood lies at the very centre of the meaning of life as God intends it to be lived. Servanthood, obedience, in the great crises of life and in the little decisions of every day, Mary saw as things of first importance. And so she doubtless taught the little boy on her lap, at her knee, through all his formative years. What greater prayer could she offer for her son than that he may grow up to be the servant of the Lord – possibly (did she glimpse it as she pondered on these things in her heart?) he might be even *the* servant of the Lord.

One of the greatest gifts that a mother can give to her children is not only to pray for them but, from the earliest years, to teach them to pray. We may be sure that Mary's little boy was not very old when he began to pray the prayer which his mother used when she first knew she was pregnant: 'I am the Lord's servant; may it be to me as you have said', or to put it more simply and shortly, 'Your will be done'. As the boy grew older, she taught him what it meant to think of God as king, to see his life under his kingship as the only life worth living. She taught him to pray: 'Your kingdom come, your will be done', and to do so, not grudgingly but exultingly.

It is not stretching our imagination too far to suggest that we owe to Mary those two basic clauses which come at the beginning of her son's prayer – 'Your kingdom come, your will be done.'

What a debt we owe her!

THE SERVANT-SON: JESUS THEN AND NOW
DONALD COGGAN

Scripture Reading

LUKE 1:26-38

In the sixth month the angel Gabriel was sent by God to a town in Galilee called Nazareth, to a virgin engaged to a man whose name was Joseph, of the house of David. The virgin's name was Mary. And he came to her and said, 'Greetings, favoured one! The Lord is with you.' But she was much perplexed by his words and pondered what sort of greeting this might be. The angel said to her, 'Do not be afraid, Mary, for you have found favour with God. And now, you will conceive in your womb and bear a son, and you will name him Jesus. He will be great, and will be called the Son of the Most High, and the Lord God will give to him the throne of his ancestor David. He will reign over the house of Jacob for ever, and of his kingdom there will be no end.' Mary said to the angel, 'How can this be, since I am a virgin?' The angel said to her, 'The Holy Spirit will come upon you, and the power of the Most High will overshadow you; therefore the child to be born will be holy; he will be called Son of God. And now, your relative Elizabeth in her old age has also conceived a son; and this is the sixth month for her who was said to be barren. For nothing will be impossible with God.' Then Mary said, 'Here am I, the servant of the Lord; let it be with me according to your word.' Then the angel departed from her.

Prayer

God, who called Mary
to motherhood and servanthood
and entrusted to her the care of your Son,
envelop us with your life, so that
in surrendering ourselves to you,
you may dwell in us
and we may dwell in you.

WEDNESDAY,
WEEK THREE

For Reflection

No Room?

It is a very sad thing to consider that on the first of two great occasions which came in his life, the national occasion of the census, our Lord was completely unnoticed; and on the second, the religious occasion of the Feast of the Passover, he was rejected and murdered.

The great God came into his world, clothed in the vesture of humanity, to take his share in that part of the world's history in which human life would be spent, and his entry was unnoticed and unknown, except by some simple shepherds, some wise men who were outside the Jewish nation altogether and a few saints like Simeon and Anna. Why was it that those people did not recognize Jesus when he came? Because their lives were so crowded with what they called religion and with all sorts of worldly things, that they could not get close to him and see him. Here is the most wonderful thing that ever happened: it is not merely a baby, though a baby is a wonderful thing enough, but God manifest as a baby, and they did not see him, they had no room for him.

In the circumstances of life, circumstances as humble as a manger, as commonplace as the carpenter's shop, and almost as tragic and awful as the Cross, he comes to us. He comes to seek and save that which is lost, to bring light to our darkness, strength to our weakness, peace to our loneliness; and we have to make a great act of faith that he really is here in our midst. The Lord is at hand. Let us try before Christmas to make room in our souls for Jesus.

We think probably too much of our coming to our Lord, and too little of his coming to us. When God came to earth, he came in disguise that only the poor and penitent and humble and the people of good will could penetrate; but when they could penetrate this disguise, there in the common straw of human poverty under the form of a child, in the dim shadows of an Eastern carpenter's shop under the form of a carpenter at his day's work, in the deep darkness of a night of sorrow under the form of a man dying in the dark – there was he of whom they were able to cry with real faith, 'Thou art the Christ, the Son of the living God!'...

That is our God, and that is what Christmas means, that the great God shrank down to the dimensions of a child to reach children, that he took quivering, suffering human flesh that he might be beaten and wounded and reveal his heart to humanity.

MEDITATIONS FOR EVERY DAY
FATHER ANDREW SDC

Scripture Reading

LUKE 2:1–7

In those days a decree went out from the Emperor Augustus that all the world should be registered. This was the first registration and was taken while Quirinius was governor of Syria. All went to their own towns to be registered. Joseph also went from the town of Nazareth in Galilee to Judea, to the city of David called Bethlehem, because he was descended from the house and family of David. He went to be registered with Mary, to whom he was engaged and who was expecting a child. While they were there the time came for her to deliver her child. And she gave birth to her firstborn son and wrapped him in bands of cloth, and laid him in a manger, because there was no place for him in the inn.

Prayer

In a manger at Bethlehem they saw Jesus.
In a carpenter's shop at Nazareth they saw Jesus.
On a cross at Calvary they saw Jesus.
In an upper room and in a garden they saw Jesus.

In the birth of a child and in the love of a parent we
see Jesus.
In our meeting with one another we see Jesus.
In our joys and in our sorrows we see Jesus.
In our doubts and questioning we see Jesus.

Seeing him, Lord, help us to love him,
to make room for him and to share our lives with
him.

THURSDAY, WEEK THREE

For Reflection

Good News!

If we are able to sing the Gloria with the angels – Glory to God in the highest, and on earth peace – and have it really mean something more than pretty tunes, then we have to know that it is good news we hear, the great glad tidings that have power to transform our lives and enable us to live, not free from fear, because we shall always have fearful times, but free of being controlled by our fear, and able to find new hope out of our suffering. That is good news that goes all the way to Easter and beyond. It is the news that says to us first of all that we are loved – without condition, without limit, beyond measure. At Christmas, the word made flesh in Jesus says 'I am for you'. Our lives are precious to God.

But that is not all. Not only are we loved. The good news of Christmas is that we can love. We know that we are far from perfect, that failure is an experience common to us all. But by grace, we are not defined by our failure. We still have space to grow in love. This is the meaning of forgiveness – our existential reality – that we are forgiven people, and that we can forgive. And as we grow in love, we will grow in courage too. Only trusting in love, in our forgiveness, in the knowledge that we are not defined by our failures, gives us courage enough to face our fears and feel our fears and know that we will come out the other side. That love is the light that shines in the darkness and will never be put out, even when we don't see anything but black. That love is eternal, and endures when all else is lost. That love replaces our childish clinging to security with a child-like trust and spontaneity.

This good news – that we are loved, that we can love – needs one thing more to make Christmas really real. It needs to be shared. Not hugged to ourselves, like a private affair, not even kept within the safety of our church walls. It needs to be told out, not in words, but in action. The word became flesh, not more words. It lived among us. We give glory to God by living good news, by being the word of love become flesh; in our healing of wounds, in our restoring of right relationships, in our struggle for justice, in our daily care-giving, in our delight in life.

Pull back the curtain on Bethlehem's stable,
strip off the tinsel and peer through the dark,
look at the child, who's a threat, yet in danger,
homeless and helpless, he first makes his mark.
Love's the secret, love's the secret,
love is God's cradle, God's table,
God's cup and God's ark.

John L. Bell

GETTING PERSONAL
KATHY GALLOWAY

Scripture Reading

LUKE 2:8–20

In that region there were shepherds living in the fields, keeping watch over their flock by night. Then an angel of the Lord stood before them, and the glory of the Lord shone around them, and they were terrified. But the angel said to them, 'Do not be afraid; for see – I am bringing you good news of great joy for all the people: to you is born this day in the city of David a Saviour, who is the Messiah, the Lord. This will be a sign for you: you will find a child wrapped in bands of cloth and lying in a manger.' And suddenly there was with the angel a multitude of the heavenly host, praising God and saying,

'Glory to God in the highest heaven,
and on earth peace among those whom he favours!'

When the angels had left them and gone into heaven, the shepherds said to one another, 'Let us now go to Bethlehem and see this thing that has taken place, which the Lord has made known to us.' So they went with haste and found Mary and Joseph, and the child lying in the manger. When they saw this, they made known what had been told them about this child; and all who heard it were amazed at what the shepherds told them. But Mary treasured all these words and pondered them in her heart. The shepherds returned glorifying and praising God for all they had heard and seen, as it had been told them.

Prayer

Jesus, Word of Love, become flesh –
heal our wounds,
grant us forgiveness,
help us in our struggles,
immerse us in your love,
that we may love as you have loved,
whatever the cost.

FRIDAY, WEEK THREE

For Reflection

Expectant Hope

How good the news must have sounded to John in his prison cell! The more we get to the heart of scripture the better we can understand that the characters we read about were all human beings just like us. John, who devoted his life to prayer and fasting to prepare people for the coming of Jesus, is apparently rewarded with incarceration and impending death. But then comes the message of hope: don't worry, everything is going to plan – death is not the end, even the dead are raised to life. 'Happy is the man who does not lose faith in me.'

As we continue to prepare for the coming of the Messiah, we too should be full of expectant hope. As we get ready to celebrate this new birth, it must happen that the word will become flesh within us, opening our eyes and ears to the wonder of what God means to us. It's ironic, really, that more than at any other time of the year we are likely to have less time for God during this hallowed season – and I speak from bitter experience. For years I have been a slave to the pride of perfection: all the Christmas cards must be sent, the parcels beautifully wrapped, and hours spent agonizing over whether so-and-so would like this or that. I have in effect spent my Advent in panic. No matter how hard I worked, so-and-so already had such and such (and I didn't send cards to the people I received them from!).

One of the ways in which we can follow John's message of repentance is to be prepared to fail, to be humble enough to opt out of what the world makes of Christmas, to make a radical pruning of our 'Christmas' activities. We need to give ourselves time to reflect on this great mystery of how it can be that almighty God can take human flesh, and as a man communicate directly to people the message of eternal life. It is a tragedy that we find ourselves preoccupied instead with tinsel and wrapping paper, running in a race against time that only ends when the key is turned on the last cash register on Christmas Eve. Twenty-four hours later all our efforts, like the wrapping paper, are torn up and forgotten and we watch the queues for the January sales assembling on our TV screens! What we're really anticipating and awaiting in joyful hope is liberation from that kind of slavery. So let us pray for the wisdom to ponder this great mystery we are about to celebrate, and to be lovingly attentive to its meaning and purpose in our lives.

A FEAST FOR ADVENT
DELIA SMITH

Scripture Reading

LUKE 7:18–23

John summoned two of his disciples and sent them to the Lord to ask, 'Are you the one who is to come, or are we to wait for another?' When the two men had come to him, they said, 'John the Baptist has sent us to you to ask, "Are you the one who is to come, or are we to wait for another?"' Jesus had just then cured many people of diseases, plagues, and evil spirits, and had given sight to many that were blind. And he answered them, 'Go and tell John what you have seen and heard: the blind receive their sight, the lame walk, the lepers are cleansed, the deaf hear, the dead are raised, the poor have good news brought to them. And blessed is anyone who takes no offence at me.'

Prayer

God of the watching and waiting ones,
God of the shepherds adoring the Babe,
God of the wise men at the end of their quest,
God of the angels giving him the glory,
God of Mary and Joseph,
God made man in Bethlehem, giving us the Word
    of love,
may we prepare for your coming
with open hearts and minds
and lovingly receive you,
the Lord of life.

SATURDAY, WEEK THREE

For Reflection

Sister Wendy Beckett (b. 1930) *is a contemplative nun, an art historian and TV presenter. This piece is taken from her book* The Gaze of Love, *which contains her commentaries on forty selected works of art, mostly contemporary.*

The Gaze of Love

The real difficulty with prayer is that it has no difficulty. Prayer is God's taking possession of us. We expose to him what we are, and he gazes on us with the creative eye of holy love. His gaze is transforming: he does not leave us in our poverty but draws into being all we are meant to become. What that is we can never know. Total Love sees us in total truth because it is only he who sees us totally. Nobody else can ever know us through and through, know why we are what we are, what inherited weaknesses and strength we have, or what wounds or insights have come to us from our upbringing. We may think that we know many of these, but we are often mistaken. We must all have had the embarrassing experience of listening to friends detail their own characteristics, and known that their verdict is not objectively true. We see one another's unconscious self-deceptions, but we may not be aware of our own. It is not only our faults we may overlook, but – perhaps even more – our virtues. There is a certain satisfaction in thinking ill of ourselves, both in that it confirms us in a hope of our lack of conceit, and in that it flatters our laziness. A gift always means we have to work with it, and so we may prefer not to be overtly aware of our own potential. But none of these escapes are possible if we pray. God sees us in our absolute truth, and seeing us, he loves us and brings us to blissful fulfilment.

How God gazes at us is not our business. We are only asked to allow him to take possession. We cannot hasten or control this state. Certainly a response is called for, but what that is to be is something that only the individual at prayer can know. There are no norms, no rules, no prohibitions, or at least, none as such. What 'rules' there are arise spontaneously in the act of prayer. All prayer demands that we look at God (which usually means that we look into 'nothingness', God being pure Spirit and unconfinable in any image), and do what seems to work. Whether our response is working or not – whether it is a way into love or an escape into self – only we can know. If it seems right, it will be right, God being bound by his own honour to make it clear to us if we are mistaken. We can see that prayer is based wholly on being truthful. If we want God to be our all, then we shall want to do whatever pleases him. Prayer is the only human action or state where cheating is impossible. As soon as pretence sets in, prayer stops. It never wholly stops since God never ceases looking at us with love, but he needs our consent if his love is not to be powerless. It is precisely this total freedom in prayer that we find so appalling. We long to be safe behind a barricade of methods, all protecting us from our own weakness, but in this very protection, shutting us off from God. It is the real self with all its weakness he desires. He cannot transform us if we insist on only offering to him our goodness, our successes, our strengths. Controlled prayer is only partial prayer: it is giving up the control to God that makes prayer true.

THE GAZE OF LOVE
SISTER WENDY BECKETT

Scripture Reading

COLOSSIANS 3:1-4, 12-14

So if you have been raised with Christ, seek the things that are above, where Christ is, seated at the right hand of God. Set your mind on things that are above, not on things that are on earth, for you have died, and your life is hidden with Christ in God. When Christ who is your life is revealed, then you will also be revealed with him in glory ... As God's chosen ones, holy and beloved, clothe yourselves with love and compassion, kindness, humility, meekness, and patience. Bear with one another and, if anyone has a complaint against another, forgive each other; just as the Lord has forgiven you, so you also must forgive. Above all, clothe yourselves with love, which binds everything together in perfect harmony.

PSALM 33:13–15

The LORD looks down from heaven;
    he sees all humankind.
From where he sits enthroned he watches
    all the inhabitants of the earth –
he who fashions the hearts of them all,
and observes all their deeds.

Prayer

Lord, You gaze on me with your love.
You come to me in your Son.
Teach me to pray with honesty and to respond humbly
to whatever you may ask of me.

THE FOURTH SUNDAY
IN ADVENT

For Reflection

John A. T. Robinson (1919–83), *after a short time in parochial ministry, taught at Wells Theological College and Clare College, Cambridge before being consecrated Bishop of Woolwich in 1959. The publication of his Honest to God led to considerable theological debate. The following quotation is from a series of his essays and addresses.*

The Invitation

The New Testament writers could not describe even the most secular events without seeing Christ meeting and judging men in them.

We cannot help using the word 'judgement' when we speak of the coming of Christ. For the world is not at ease when he is present – and that is hardly surprising after what it has done to him. No wonder the Bible pictures people as trying to hide their faces from him.

But it shows us another side as well. There is one place – in the fellowship of the Church – where it pictures men actually inviting him to come. 'Our Lord, come!' (1 Corinthians 16:22); 'Come, Lord Jesus!' (Revelation 22:20). 'Come and stand in the midst of thy disciples and make thyself known in the breaking of the bread.'

Such was the call of the early Christians. For them too he was not simply someone who was to come again at the end of time. He was someone who kept coming in, someone they knew and met as he stood among them in their worship week by week. 'Behold, I stand at the door and knock; if any one hears my voice and opens the door, I will come in and eat with him, and he with me' (Revelation 3:20). 'It is the Lord!' (John 21:7). To the disciples their returning Lord was a figure of joy. And ever since Christians have been eager to meet with him, to welcome him to their midst, to know his presence among them.

Suppose he came back? Christians have no need to suppose. They know he comes back – and pre-eminently as he meets with them at his own board. For this is the point above all where Christ promised his returning presence to his friends. It is as though he said, 'You may meet me anywhere; but here you will meet me and I shall meet you'.

But this particular meeting-point is but to prepare us to meet him at all points. Shall we know him when he comes? Shall we recognize his knock? That depends very largely on whether we have already got to know him and made him welcome in our lives. Shall we be able to see the moral issue in tomorrow's headlines, shall we be able next time to see the person behind the skin? And if we do so, can we face it, can we face him? That depends on whether we are used to looking for Christ, on whether we expect him to be there and count on him coming in. And all these choices build up, and make us by the way we choose the sort of people we shall be when finally we have to face him – that Man whom we have either learnt to live with and to love, or from whom we have turned away, on this occasion, or this, or that.

ON BEING THE CHURCH IN THE WORLD
JOHN A. T. ROBINSON

Scripture Reading

REVELATION 3:20–22

'Listen! I am standing at the door, knocking; if you hear my voice and open the door, I will come in to you and eat with you, and you with me. To the one who conquers I will give a place with me on my throne, just as I myself conquered and sat down with my Father on his throne. Let anyone who has an ear listen to what the Spirit is saying to the churches.'

REVELATION 22:17

The Spirit and the bride say, 'Come'.
And let everyone who hears say, 'Come.'
And let everyone who is thirsty come.
Let anyone who wishes take the water of life as a gift.

REVELATION 22:20

The one who testifies to these things says, 'Surely I am coming soon!' Amen. Come, Lord Jesus!

Prayer

O Lord, give us yourself above all things.
It is in your coming alone that we are enriched.
It is in your coming that true gifts come.
Come, Lord, that we may share the gifts of your
    Presence.
Come, Lord, with healing of the past,
come and calm our memories.
Come with joy for the present,
come and give life to our existence.
Come with hope for the future,
come and give a sense of eternity.
Come with strength for our wills,
come with power for our thoughts.
Come with love for our heart,
come and give affection to our being.
Come, Lord, give yourself above all things,
and help us to give ourselves to you.

TIDES AND SEASONS
DAVID ADAM

MONDAY, WEEK FOUR

For Reflection

Dietrich Bonhoeffer (1906–45), a Protestant Lutheran pastor and theologian, was active in German resistance against Nazism. He was arrested and eventually executed at Flossenbürg concentration camp. He wrote extensively on subjects of theological interest. One of his notable books, The Cost of Discipleship, is a study of the Sermon on the Mount in which he argues for greater spiritual discipline.

Christmas in Prison

You can't help thinking of my being in prison over Christmas, and it is bound to throw a shadow over the few hours of happiness which will await you in these times. All I can do to help is to assure you that I know you will keep it in the same spirit as I do, for we are agreed on how Christmas ought to be kept. How could it be otherwise when my attitude to Christmas is a heritage I owe to you? I need not tell you how much I long to be released and to see you all again. But for years you have given us such lovely Christmasses, that our grateful memories are strong enough to cast their rays over a darker one. In times like these we learn as never before what it means to possess a past and a spiritual heritage untrammelled by the changes and chances of the present. A spiritual heritage reaching back for centuries is a wonderful support and comfort in face of all the temporary stresses and strains. I believe that the man who is aware of such reserves of power need not be ashamed of the tender feelings evoked by the memory of a rich and noble past, for such feelings belong in my opinion to the better and nobler part of mankind. They will not overwhelm those who hold fast to values of which no man can deprive them.

For a Christian there is nothing peculiarly difficult about Christmas in a prison cell. I daresay it will have more meaning and will be observed with greater sincerity here in this prison than in places where all that survives of the feast is its name. That misery, suffering, poverty, loneliness, helplessness and guilt look very different to the eyes of God from what they do to man, that God should come down to the very place which men usually abhor, that Christ was born in a stable because there was no room for him in the inn – these are things which a prisoner can understand better than anyone else. For him the Christmas story is glad tidings in a very real sense. And that faith gives him a part in the communion of saints, a fellowship transcending the bounds of time and space and reducing the months of confinement here to insignificance.

On Christmas Eve I shall be thinking of you all very much, and I want you to believe that I too shall have a few hours of real joy and that I am not allowing my troubles to get the better of me.

LETTERS AND PAPERS FROM PRISON
DIETRICH BONHOEFFER

Scripture Reading

PHILIPPIANS 4:4–9

Rejoice in the Lord always; again I will say, Rejoice. Let your gentleness be known to everyone. The Lord is near. Do not worry about anything, but in everything by prayer and supplication with thanksgiving let your requests be made known to God. And the peace of God, which surpasses all understanding, will keep your hearts and your minds in Christ Jesus.

Finally, beloved, whatever is true, whatever is honourable, whatever is just, whatever is pure, whatever is pleasing, whatever is commendable, if there is any excellence and if there is anything worthy of praise, think about these things. Keep on doing the things that you have learned and received and heard and seen in me, and the God of peace will be with you.

Prayer

God of our joys and sorrows,
you made your home among us;
comfort and console the prisoner,
be with the oppressed, the exile and the wounded.
Give us compassionate hearts
and bring us all to the joys of heaven,
our true home,
where you live and reign,
Father, Son and Holy Spirit.

TUESDAY, WEEK FOUR

For Reflection

Jane Williams (b. 1957) *is a freelance writer and theologian who taught doctrine and history at Trinity Theological College, Bristol. A visiting lecturer at King's College, London, she is assistant dean and lecturer at St Mellitus College.* Approaching Christmas *is the companion volume to* Approaching Easter.

Word Made Flesh

Imagining the details of Jesus' birth has been a popular pastime for much of Christian history. The mystery plays that were performed in the Middle Ages, for example, import all kinds of extra characters, like a midwife to help Mary with the birth. But the Gospel writers just stick to the bare bones of the story. They want us to get a sense of what is happening here, of the contrast between the magnitude of what God is doing and the very ordinary methods used to accomplish it.

It is St John's Gospel that really brings out the meaning that the others hint at. Like Luke, John hardly mentions the birth of the child, but he leaves us in no doubt about what is going on.

The birth is summed up in one phrase: 'the Word became flesh' – a human being. John wants us to picture the Word, living in power with God the Father, creating the world, the source of all its life. This is what becomes flesh. The extraordinary power that enabled the whole universe is suddenly contained in a human baby. John wants us to feel the shock of that, to make our imagination reel as we try to think of what that means.

But, if John starts with the big picture – the creative life of God – Christians believe that at Christmas God starts with the small picture. A child is something we can understand. A human baby is a symbol of life and hope. Each new human life is miraculous. A whole new person comes into existence.

The little commonplace miracle of birth is something we almost take for granted. But in the birth of the baby Jesus, this is what God is offering over and over again. This is an integral part of the nature of God, to make new life. That is why there is any life at all, because the creator of the universe is so full of life that it pours out into the world. God is always lifegiving, and the birth of Jesus is God's offer of new life. A baby starts the world with a clean slate. It can discover its own character. It can interact with what is around it and experience and change and grow. In Jesus, God offers us the chance to start a new life, as though we were born again as babies. We can be born into the family of God and learn from that family environment. Life is natural to God, who does not begrudge it to us or force it on to us. But as we look at the baby Jesus with love and compassion, God hopes we might see that we are longing to be always what we are in that moment. Just like the few people at

Midnight Mass in the quiet country church, or the weeping girl by the seaside, as we look at that baby we are touched. We long to feel that we might change into the kind of people who could always sense the presence of the angels and respond with love and kindness to the world around us. And at Christmas, God says, 'Nothing is impossible.'

APPROACHING CHRISTMAS
JANE WILLIAMS

Scripture Reading

JOHN 1:1-5, 14

In the beginning was the Word, and the Word was with God, and the Word was God. He was in the beginning with God. All things came into being through him, and without him not one thing came into being. What has come into being in him was life, and the life was the light of all people. The light shines in the darkness, and the darkness did not overcome it ... And the Word became flesh and lived among us, and we have seen his glory, the glory as of a father's only son, full of grace and truth.

Prayer

Thank you, dear Lord, for the gift of life.
Forgive us for taking it for granted.
Thank you for entering into this life as one of us,
for showing us the pattern of true living
in your Son, Jesus.
Thank you for family life.
We commend to you all who feel unloved,
for those separated from loved ones,
the lonely and the oppressed,
the wounded and injured,
the exploited and manipulated.
May they know your love
and the assurance that with you nothing is impossible.

WEDNESDAY,
WEEK FOUR

For Reflection

Justin Welby (b. 1956) is the 105th Archbishop of Canterbury. Formerly Rector of Southam, Warwickshire, in 2002 he was appointed canon residentiary and co-director of Coventry Cathedral's International Centre for Reconciliation. He was the Dean of Liverpool from 2007 until 2011, then served as the Bishop of Durham for just over a year before being enthroned as Archbishop of Canterbury in 2013.

Good News of Great Joy

The Christmas story could be told simply with a happy ending where the Gospel reading ended. 'Shepherds are cold, shepherds see angels, shepherds head into town and see baby, and shepherds disappear into sunrise, happy.' If we ended there, Christmas removes us from reality. Christmas becomes something utterly remote, about lives entirely different, fictional, naïve, tidy. That's not Christmas. Jesus came to the reality of this world to transform that reality – not to take us into some fantasy kind of 'happy ever after' but to bring 'good news of great joy for all people'.

It is good news precisely because God addresses the world as it is. Isaiah speaks of warriors and garments rolled in blood, of yokes on people's shoulders, of oppression. We know that story; it is the lived reality of so many suffering today. Yet Isaiah announces the news of God bringing light, joy, and exultation, through a child!

It is 'good news of great joy' because a helpless baby (who is God) becomes the one who changes this world decisively. Differently to any other figure in human history, Jesus breaks in, not to help us escape, but to transform and take hold of our past, our present and our future. This baby brings the promise of forgiveness, the certainty of love and the hope of peace.

This means that whilst we must truly face the state of the world to which Jesus came, we can – we must – be equally realistic about the difference it makes.

Jesus did not come for one day. Jesus changed things for ever.

He comes to the person who turns and calls to him, bringing forgiveness and new life. That is an offer to all of us today, whether full of the joy of Christmas or in the midst of a personal darkness of despair and hopelessness. If Jesus can be laid in a manger there is nowhere that is not fitting for him to come, no person who is unfit to receive him.

He comes to the person nearing death, whether that death is premature or after a long life, and he brings assurance of his presence, and the hope of eternity. Jesus is the promise that 'God is with us', no matter what.

To the region caught up in war or to the family caught up in fights, he offers a transformation of hearts so there might be reconciliation. He offers a stepping out of the trenches, away from positions taken against enemies and into new paths of relating.

He comes to lives that can too easily be caught up in acquiring, amassing, consuming and self-obsessing, bringing a shift in our horizon – beyond ourselves, to those who don't have what we have. If we hear this story properly we look away from ourselves, from our life with its care and burdens. This is freedom: as our perspective widens, so we are healed. This is good news of great joy for all people...

Yet because Jesus comes as a child, as baby, we are not manipulated or forced, we have freedom to choose whether we hear his story properly or not. This baby is love so fierce it changes universes, love so gentle that the weakest is free to choose.

Rowan Williams puts it beautifully in his poem 'Advent Calendar',

> He will come, will come,
> will come like crying in the night,
> like blood, like breaking,
> as the earth writhes to toss him free.
> He will come like a child.

Jesus does not remove us from reality, he indwells it; and he indwells us if we invite him. To be indwelt by Christ changes our understanding of reality, so that with his eyes we may see the world and love it, overflowing with the love that he gives to us...

What an extraordinary God this is who makes all the difference in the world. Don't we all long for his reality rather than our make-believe? The question is whether we will have open hands and ears, hearts and lives to receive him, not just on Christmas Day, but each day of our lives.

More than that, having received him, whether we will make it our life's aim – like the shepherds – for the sake of his world to be the difference Jesus came to bring.

CHRISTMAS SERMON 2014
JUSTIN WELBY

Scripture Reading

ISAIAH 9:2-7

The people who walked in darkness
    have seen a great light;
those who lived in a land of deep darkness –
    on them light has shined.
You have multiplied the nation,
    you have increased its joy;
they rejoice before you
    as with joy at the harvest,
    as people exult when dividing plunder.
For the yoke of their burden,
    and the bar across their shoulders,
    the rod of their oppressor,
    you have broken as on the day of Midian.
For all the boots of the tramping warriors

and all the garments rolled in blood
    shall be burned as fuel for the fire.
For a child has been born for us,
    a son given to us;
authority rests upon his shoulders;
    and he is named
Wonderful Counsellor, Mighty God,
    Everlasting Father, Prince of Peace.
His authority shall grow continually,
    and there shall be endless peace
for the throne of David and his kingdom.
    He will establish and uphold it
with justice and with righteousness
    from this time onwards and for evermore.
The zeal of the LORD of hosts will do this.

Prayer

Into a world of sin and shame,
of war and waste
of pain and loss
the Saviour Christ was born.
Into a world that's just the same
he's born again today.
This is the real world, the harsh world
he came to save.

This is my world of which I am but a small part.
Come and live in me, that I might live with you,
Jesus, Child of Bethlehem.

THURSDAY,
WEEK FOUR

For Reflection

Hope in a Dark World

'A shoot shall sprout from the stump of Jesse, and from his roots a bud shall blossom. The spirit of the LORD shall rest upon him...'

These words have stayed with me during the day. Our salvation comes from something small, tender, and vulnerable, something hardly noticeable. God, who is the Creator of the Universe, comes to us in smallness, weakness, and hiddenness.

I find this a hopeful message. Somehow, I keep expecting loud and impressive events to convince me and others of God's saving power, but over and over again I am reminded that spectacles, power plays, and big events are the ways of the world. Our temptation is to be distracted by them and made blind to the 'shoot that shall sprout from the stump'.

When I have no eyes for the small signs of God's presence – the smile of a baby, the carefree play of children, the words of encouragement and gestures of love offered by friends – I will always remain tempted to despair.

The small child of Bethlehem, the unknown young man of Nazareth, the rejected preacher, the naked man on the cross, *he* asks for my full attention. The work of our salvation takes place in a world that continues to shout, scream, and overwhelm us with its claims and promises. But the promise is hidden in the shoot and sprouts from the stump, a shoot that hardly anyone notices.

I remember seeing a film on the human misery and devastation brought by the bomb on Hiroshima. Among all the scenes of terror and despair emerged one image of a man quietly writing a word in calligraphy. All his attention was directed to writing that one word. That image made this gruesome film a hopeful film. Isn't that what God is doing? Writing the divine word of hope in the midst of our dark world?

SEEDS OF HOPE
HENRI J. M. NOUWEN

Scripture Reading

ISAIAH 11:1-5

> A shoot shall come out from the stock of Jesse,
>   and a branch shall grow out of its roots.
> The spirit of the Lord shall rest on him,
>   the spirit of wisdom and understanding,
>   the spirit of counsel and might,
>   the spirit of the knowledge and the fear of the
>   LORD.
> His delight shall be in the fear of the Lord.

He shall not judge by what his eyes see,
    or decide by what his ears hear;
but with righteousness he shall judge the poor,
    and decide with equity for the meek of the earth...
Righteousness shall be the belt around his waist,
    and faithfulness the belt around his loins.

Prayer

Lord, fill my heart with your goodness.
Dwell in me and let me know your peace.
Enter into the dark places of my life
that I may overflow with your love
and reflect your forgiveness,
    bringing forth the fruits of love, hope, joy and peace.

FRIDAY, WEEK FOUR

For Reflection

Steve Brady *is Principal of Moorlands College, Dorset, where he also teaches Theology and New Testament Greek. His books include* King of Heaven, Lord of Earth, All You Need Is Christ *and* Affirming Your Faith.

Dwelling Among Us

Theologians have endlessly debated the background of the phrase 'the Word'. Is it to be understood from its use in Greek philosophy or Old Testament thought? What is clear is that God has eternally been able to express himself, and that creative expression is not merely a thought but a person: 'In the beginning was the Word, and the Word was with God, and the Word was God' (John 1:1). Here the Word's eternity, closest proximity to the Father and own essential deity are all asserted. There never was a time when the Word was not, and that Word became 'flesh', a real human being. Many people baulk at the truth claims of Christianity, involving miracles, Jesus as the way to God, his resurrection and so on. But here is the greatest miracle of all – God becoming man. As Queen Lucy puts it in C. S. Lewis' book *The Last Battle*, 'a Stable once had something inside it that was bigger than our whole world'. If that is true, then turning water into wine, healing the sick, calming the storms and raising the dead are the very things we would expect of an incarnate God.

It would be easy to overlook the depth of humility contained in the phrase 'made his dwelling among us'. Who has not enjoyed hearing the stories of some of life's great entrepreneurs and others who have risen via rags to riches? But in Jesus we see the divine paradox. It is a 'riches to rags' story being played out. He who was 'at the Father's side' as 'the true light' of God, who enjoyed the company of angels and spirits purer than we can conceive, stepped into our darkness, stooping to join the human race. In coming to save the world, Jesus changed addresses and became one of us. Likewise, since then, the incarnation principle – coming to where people are – has been at the heart of all true Christian mission to the world. Our missionaries like J. Hudson Taylor, who spent over 50 years in China, have followed Christ's example, changing locations, learning a foreign language, adopting local customs and clothing, in order to bring good news to the world.

Let us rejoice this Christmas that God's eternal Son, his One and Only, 'full of grace and truth', has brought light for our darkness and hope for our despair.

THE INCREDIBLE JOURNEY
STEVE BRADY

Scripture Reading

JOHN 1:14–18

And the Word became flesh and lived among us, and we have seen his glory, the glory as of a father's only son, full of grace and truth. (John testified to him and cried out, 'This was he of whom I said, "He who comes after me ranks ahead of me because he was before me." ') From his fullness we have all received, grace upon grace. The law indeed was given through Moses, grace and truth came through Jesus Christ. No one has ever seen God. It is God the only Son, who is close to the Father's heart, who has made him known.

Prayer

God of hope,
be with us on our Advent journey
to the stable and beyond,
be with us in our meeting
and in our travelling together.
Be with us on our Advent journey
to the stable and beyond,
our God of hope.

JOHN BIRCH

CHRISTMAS EVE

For Reflection

This Holy Night

How shall I describe this holy night? How shall I give expression to the multitude of feelings and ideas that come together in this most joyful celebration? This night is the fulfilment of four weeks of expectation; it is the remembrance of the most intimate mystery of life, the birth of God in an agonizing world; it is the planting of the seeds of compassion, freedom and peace in a harsh, unfree, and hateful society; it is hope in a new earth to come. It is all that and much, much more. For me it is also the end of a most blessed and graceful retreat and the beginning of a new life. A step out of silence into the many sounds of the world, out of the cloister into the unkept garden without hedges or boundaries. In many ways I feel as though I have received a small, vulnerable child in my arms and have been asked to carry him with me out of the intimacy of the monastery into a world waiting for light to come.

This day is the day in which I will experience not only the beauty of the night with songs of peace but also the wide ocean stretching out between two continents. This day the smallness and vulnerability of the child and the vastness of our earth will both enter my soul. I know that without the child, I have no reason to live but also that without a growing awareness of the suffering of humanity, I will not fulfil the call that the child has given me...

What can I say of a night like this? It is all very small and very large, very close and very distant, very tangible and very elusive. I keep thinking about the Christmas scene that Anthony arranged under the altar. This probably is the most beautiful 'crib' I have ever seen. Three small wood-carved figures made in India: a poor woman, a poor man, and a small child between them. The carving is simple, nearly primitive. No eyes, no ears, no mouths, just the contours of the faces. The figures are smaller than a human hand – nearly too small to attract attention at all. But then – a beam of light shines on the three figures and projects large shadows on the wall of the sanctuary. That says it all. The light thrown on the smallness of Mary, Joseph, and the Child projects them as large, hopeful shadows against the walls of our life and our world. While looking at the intimate scene we already see the first outlines of the majesty and glory they represent. While witnessing the most human of human events, I see the majesty of God appearing on the horizon of my existence. While being moved by the gentleness of these three people, I am already awed by the immense greatness of God's love appearing in my world. Without the radiant beam of light shining into the darkness there is little to be seen. I might just pass by these three simple people and continue to walk in darkness. But everything changes with the light...

The light has made me see not only the three small figures but also their huge shadows far away. This light makes all things new and reveals the greatness hidden in the small event of this holy night. I pray that I will have the strength to keep the light alive in my heart so that I can see and point to the promising shadows appearing on the walls of our world.

THE GENESEE DIARY
HENRI J. M. NOUWEN

Scripture Reading

MICAH 5:2-5

But you, O Bethlehem of Ephrathah,
    who are one of the little clans of Judah,
from you shall come forth for me
    one who is to rule in Israel,
whose origin is from of old,
    from ancient days.
Therefore he shall give them up until the time
    when she who is in labour has brought forth;
then the rest of his brethren shall return
    to the people of Israel.
And he shall stand and feed his flock in the strength
    of the LORD,
    in the majesty of the name of the LORD his God.
And they shall live secure, for now he shall be great
    to the ends of the earth;
and he shall be the one of peace.

Prayer

Lord Jesus, Light of the world,
overcoming the darkness of fear and doubt.
As we celebrate your birth
in the company of Mary and Joseph,
may we begin to see the world emerging from
    the shadows
with new hope and joy.

As you chose the poor and lowly,
the outcast and marginalized
to receive the Good News,
so may we worship you with angels and shepherds
in the meekness of our hearts.

As we draw near to Bethlehem
we pray for its people
that they may know the peace of the Child born in
    their midst
and may share with us and all people
the joy of this holy night.

CHRISTMAS DAY

For Reflection

Brian D. McLaren (b. 1956) is an internationally acclaimed speaker who has been named in Time magazine as one of the most influential Evangelical Christians of today. His books have been translated into many languages and he is a frequent guest on TV and Radio in the USA. His We Make the Road by Walking (2014) has been described as a 'turn towards constructive and practical theology'.

The Light and the Life

What do we mean when we say Jesus is the light? Just as a glow on the eastern horizon tells us that a long night is almost over, Jesus' birth signals the beginning of the end for a dark night of fear, hostility, violence and the greed that has descended on our world. Jesus' birth signals the start of a new day, a new way, a new understanding of what it means to be alive.

Aliveness, he will teach, is a gift available to all by God's grace. It flows not from taking but from giving, not from fear but from faith, not from conflict but from reconciliation, not from domination, but from service. It isn't found in the outward trappings of religion – rules and rituals, controversies and scruples, temples and traditions. No, it springs from our innermost being like a fountain of living water. It intoxicates us like the best wine ever and so turns life from a disappointment into a banquet. This new light of aliveness and love opens us up to rethink everything – to go back and become like little children again. Then we can rediscover the world with a fresh, child-like wonder – seeing the world in new light, the light of Christ.

At Christmas, then, we remember a silent, holy night long ago when Luke tells us of a young and very pregnant woman and a weary man walking beside her. They had travelled over eighty miles, a journey of several days, from Nazareth in the province of Galilee to Bethlehem in the province of Judea. Mary went into labour, and because nobody could provide them with a normal bed in a normal house, she had to give birth in a stable. We can imagine oxen and donkeys and cattle filling the air with their sounds and scent as Mary wrapped the baby in rags and laid him in a manger, a food trough for farm animals. On that dark night, in such a humble place, enfleshed in a tiny, vulnerable, homeless, helpless baby ... God's light began to glow.

Politicians compete for the highest offices. Business tycoons scramble for a bigger and bigger piece of the pie. Armies march and scientists study and philosophers philosophize and preachers preach and labourers sweat. But in the silent baby, lying in that humble manger, there pulses more potential power and wisdom and grace and aliveness than all the rest of us can imagine.

To be alive in the adventure of Jesus is to kneel at the manger and gaze upon the little baby who is radiant with so much promise for our world today.

So let us light a candle for the Christ child, for the infant Jesus, the Word made flesh. Let our hearts glow with that light that was in him, so that we become candles through which his light shines still. For Christmas is a process as well as an event. Your heart and mine can become the little town, the stable, the manger ... even now. Let a new day, a new creation, a new you, a new me, begin. Let there be light.

WE MAKE THE ROAD BY WALKING
BRIAN D. MCLAREN

Scripture Reading

JOHN 1:3–5
What has come into being in him was life, and the life was the light of all people. The light shines in the darkness, and the darkness did not overcome it.

JOHN 8:12
'I am the light of the world. Whoever follows me will never walk in darkness but will have the light of life.'

Prayer

Today we enter the stable at Bethlehem
to worship you, Lord Christ,
to praise you,
to give you the glory.

With angels and archangels
and all the company of heaven,
with family and friends
and all peoples, we raise our cry:
Holy, Holy, Holy to the One
who came, who comes
and who will come.

ACKNOWLEDGEMENTS

Advent Sunday

Extract from *The Coming of God* by Sister Maria Boulding (2001), published by Canterbury Press, used by permission of Stanbrook Abbey.

Monday, Week One

Extract from *The Genesee Diary* by Henri J. M. Nouwen (1995), published by Darton, Longman & Todd. Extract from *Power Lines* by David Adam (1992), published by SPCK, used by permission.

Tuesday, Week One

Extract from *Meditations for Every* Day by Father Andrew SDC.

Wednesday, Week One

Extract from *The Crown of the Year* by Austin Farrer.

Thursday, Week One

Extract from *A Feast for Advent* by Delia Smith (1996), published by BRF, used by permission.

Friday, Week One

Extract from *Getting Personal* by Kathy Galloway (1995), published by SPCK, used by permission.

ACKNOWLEDGEMENTS

Saturday, Week One

Extract from *Stars and Angels* by Michael Stancliffe (1997), published by Canterbury Press, used by permission of Hymns Ancient and Modern Ltd.

The Second Sunday in Advent

Extract from *The Compassionate Quest* by Trystan Owain Hughes (2013), published by SPCK, used by permission.

Monday, Week Two

Extract from *Candles in the Dark* by David Adam (2004), © Kevin Mayhew Ltd, used by permission.

Tuesday, Week Two

Extract from *The Coming of God* by Sister Maria Boulding (2001), published by Canterbury Press, used by permission of Stanbrook Abbey.

Wednesday, Week Two

Extract from *Take the Plunge* by Timothy Radcliffe OP (2012), published by Continuum, an imprint of Bloomsbury Publishing Plc.

Thursday, Week Two

Two extracts from *Tides and Seasons* by David Adam (1989), published by SPCK, used by permission.

Friday, Week Two

Extract from *Being Christian* by Rowan Williams (2014), published by SPCK, used by permission.

Saturday, Week Two

Extract from *Pilgrimage* by Andrew Jones (2011), published by BRF, used by permission.

The Third Sunday in Advent

Extract from *What Is the Point of Being a Christian?* by Timothy Radcliffe OP (2005), published by Continuum, an imprint of Bloomsbury Publishing Plc.

Monday, Week Three

Extract from *When the Time Was Right* by Stephen Rand (2006), published by BRF, reproduced by kind permission of Stephen Rand.

Tuesday, Week Three

Extract from *The Servant-Son* by Donald Coggan (1995), published by SPCK, used by permission.

Wednesday, Week Three

Extract from *Meditations for Every Day* by Father Andrew SDC.

Thursday, Week Three

Extract from *Getting Personal* by Kathy Galloway (1995), published by SPCK, used by permission.

ACKNOWLEDGEMENTS

Friday, Week Three

Extract from *A Feast for Advent* by Delia Smith (1996), published by BRF, used by permission.

Saturday, Week Three

Extract from *The Gaze of Love* by Sister Wendy Beckett, © 1993. Used by permission of Zondervan. All rights reserved.

The Fourth Sunday in Advent

Extract from *On Being the Church in the World* by John A. T. Robinson (2013), published by SCM Press, used by permission of Hymns Ancient and Modern Ltd. Extract from *Tides and Seasons* by David Adam (1989), published by SPCK, used by permission.

Monday, Week Four

Extract from *Letters and Papers from Prison* by Dietrich Bonhoeffer (1971), published by SCM Press, used by permission of Hymns Ancient and Modern Ltd.

Tuesday, Week Four

Extract from *Approaching Christmas* by Jane Williams (2012), published by Lion Books, 2005, 2012. © 2005 Jane Williams. Used with permission of Lion Hudson plc.

Wednesday, Week Four

Extract from Christmas Sermon 2014 by Archbishop Justin Welby, http://www.archbishopofcanterbury.org/

articles.php/5469/archbishop-of-canterburys-christmas-sermon

Thursday, Week Four

Extract from *Seeds of Hope* by Henri J. M. Nouwen (1989), published by Darton, Longman & Todd.

Friday, Week Four

Extract from *The Incredible Journey* by Steve Brady (2011), published by BRF, used by permission. Prayer by John Birch, used by permission.

Christmas Eve

Extract from *The Genesee Diary* by Henri J. M. Nouwen (1995), published by Darton, Longman & Todd.

Christmas Day

Extract from *We Make the Road by Walking: A Year-Long Quest for Spiritual Formation, Reorientation, and Activation* by Brian D. McLaren (2014). © 2014 Brian D. McLaren. Used by permission of Jericho Books, an imprint of Faith Words/Hachette Book Group USA Inc.

While every effort has been made to trace the owners of copyright material reproduced herein, the author and publishers would like to apologise for any omissions and will be pleased to incorporate missing acknowledgements in any future editions.

INDEX OF AUTHORS